About This Book

Why Is This Topic Important?

Training encompasses more than planned off-the-job learning experiences. Most training and workplace learning occurs *in real time* and *on the job*—not *off the job* or *away from work*. That is true whether the employer is a venerable and financially secure member of the elite Fortune 500 or is a recently founded, and perhaps even financially strapped, small business. On-the-job training (OJT) is perhaps most critical in small to medium-sized organizations lacking the staff, the internal expertise, or the other resources to conduct planned training or maintain a cadre of training professionals. Yet it is often ignored, since some employers have a bias toward glitzy, expensive, technologically driven solutions to training problems.

What Can You Achieve with This Book?

Simply stated, this book provides everything you need to think through how to install a low-cost, low-tech approach to improving real-time work performance by installing a planned on-the-job training program in an organization.

How Is This Book Organized?

A pretest opens the book. It should help employers assess the status of OJT in their organizations. It also serves as an advance organizer of the book's contents.

The book is organized into three parts. *Part One* consists of Chapters One through Four and is entitled "Foundations of OJT: Building an Effective Organizational Climate to Support OJT." *Part Two* consists of Chapters Five through Ten and is entitled "Preparing and Delivering OJT." *Part Three* consists of Chapter Eleven. It is entitled "Reflections on OJT."

Chapter One lays the book's foundation by explaining why OJT is important, briefly reviewing what has been written about it, listing major barriers to its effective use, and offering ideas for overcoming those barriers. Chapter Two offers guidance for establishing an OJT program. Chapter Three reviews key management issues that should be addressed during program start-up. Chapter Four describes methods of training the trainers and learners for their roles in OJT and on-the-job learning (OJL).

Chapters Five through Ten comprise the core of this book. They are based on DAPPER, a model for OJT and an acronym made up of the first letters of steps in the planned OJT process. Chapter Five is thus about discovering needs for planned OJT. Chapter Six is about analyzing work, worker, and workplace for OJT. Chapter Seven is about preparing planned OJT. Chapter Eight is about presenting planned OJT. Chapter Nine centers around evaluating the results of OJT, and Chapter Ten is about reviewing aids to planned OJT. Chapter Eleven emphasizes six key lessons about successful planned OJT programs.

The book concludes with a glossary that defines key terms used throughout the book and a list of resources for the reader's future use. Finally, the CD-ROM that accompanies this book provides all worksheets appearing in the book and also contains an entire train-the-trainer workshop on OJT, complete with reproducible slides, a participant workbook, and a leader's guide.

About Pfeiffer

Pfeiffer serves the professional development and hands-on resource needs of training and human resource practitioners and gives them products to do their jobs better. We deliver proven ideas and solutions from experts in HR development and HR management, and we offer effective and customizable tools to improve workplace performance. From novice to seasoned professional, Pfeiffer is the source you can trust to make yourself and your organization more successful.

Essential Knowledge Pfeiffer produces insightful, practical, and comprehensive materials on topics that matter the most to training and HR professionals. Our Essential Knowledge resources translate the expertise of seasoned professionals into practical, how-to guidance on critical workplace issues and problems. These resources are supported by case studies, worksheets, and job aids and are frequently supplemented with CD-ROMs, websites, and other means of making the content easier to read, understand, and use.

Essential Tools Pfeiffer's Essential Tools resources save time and expense by offering proven, ready-to-use materials—including exercises, activities, games, instruments, and assessments—for use during a training or team-learning event. These resources are frequently offered in looseleaf or CD-ROM format to facilitate copying and customization of the material.

Pfeiffer also recognizes the remarkable power of new technologies in expanding the reach and effectiveness of training. While e-hype has often created whizbang solutions in search of a problem, we are dedicated to bringing convenience and enhancements to proven training solutions. All our e-tools comply with rigorous functionality standards. The most appropriate technology wrapped around essential content yields the perfect solution for today's on-the-go trainers and human resource professionals.

Pfeiffer
www.pfeiffer.com

Essential resources for training and HR professionals

Praise for *Improving On-the-Job Training*

"An excellent contribution to the field, this book offers a realistic, practical focus on OJT, which is probably the most common form of training. It's too easy for people to think that OJT is simple, when in fact success with OJT is elusive. This book will show you how to do it. *Improving On-the-Job Training* will show practitioners how to establish and run an effective OJT program."

—Timothy W. Spannaus, research fellow,
Institute for Learning and Performance
Improvement, senior lecturer,
Instructional Technology,
Wayne State University

"As we expand our businesses, we will need workers to perform more complex tasks effectively. This book gives us an excellent model to implement OJT in real time and in real workplaces to create a high- performance workforce."

—William H. Lowthert,
leadership development manager,
PPL Susquehanna

"Rothwell, a world-renowned training expert, addresses one of the most critical areas of training used by all businesses and is also the most common form of training, on-the-job training. This book will provide an invaluable tool for any business to use to systematically develop successful OJT programs. The information in this book will assist companies in improving their performance and productivity through the proven methods recommended by William Rothwell."

—Patrick E. Gerity, executive director,
Office of Corporate Partnerships,
Slippery Rock University

"I was in the technical training business for over 30 years, 19 as the technical training manager for a Fortune 500 company before retiring. In all these years I've have seen many new approaches to training, but in reviewing all the new methods it still comes down to the most successful way of training especially hands-on and that is on-the-job training. This book provides a step-by-step practical methodology to improve performance. If companies would just follow the concepts in this book and adhere to them, training would be a normal part of an operation and the need for justification would no longer exist."

—Joseph A. Benkowski, associate dean outreach,
University of Wisconsin-Stout

William J. Rothwell dedicates this book to his wife, Marcelina Rothwell.

H.C. Kazanas dedicates this book to his wife, Nuria Kazanas.

IMPROVING ON-THE-JOB TRAINING

How to Establish and Operate a Comprehensive OJT Program

SECOND EDITION

William J. Rothwell
H.C. Kazanas

www.pfeiffer.com

Library of Congress Cataloging-in-Publication Data

Rothwell, William J.
Improving on-the-job training: how to establish and operate a
comprehensive OJT program / William J. Rothwell, H. C. Kazanas.—2nd ed.
p. cm.
Includes bibliographical references and index.

ISBN 0-7879-6505-7 (alk. paper)
1. Employees—Training of. I. Kazanas, H. C. II. Title.
HF5549.5.T7R658 2004
658.3'124—dc22
2003022397

Acquiring Editor: Matthew Davis
Director of Development: Kathleen Dolan Davies
Developmental Editor: Susan Rachmeler
Editor: Rebecca Taff
Senior Production Editor: Dawn Kilgore
Manufacturing Supervisor: Bill Matherly

Printing 10 9 8 7 6 5 4 3 2 1

CONTENTS

PART THREE: REFLECTIONS ON OJT   141

TABLES, FIGURES, & EXHIBITS

Tables

Figures

Exhibits

CONTENTS OF THE CD-ROM

Selected Worksheets and Resources from the Book

Improving On-the-Job Training: A Fully Customizable Leader Guide for a Train-the-Trainer Program

Improving On-the-Job Training: A Fully Customizable Participant Guide for a Train-the-Trainer Program

Slides to Accompany *Improving On-the-Job Training*

INTRODUCTION

Getting the Most From This Resource

The word *training* continues to evoke a mental image of group-based rather than on-the-job learning or online learning experiences for most people. That is particularly true in major corporations in which training enjoys high visibility and has been effectively integrated with human resource planning, employee selection, job design, organization design, organization development, and compensation and benefits.

Of course, training encompasses more than planned off-the-job learning experiences. Most training and workplace learning occurs *in real time* and *on the job* —not *off the job* or *away from work*. That is true whether the employer is a venerable and financially secure member of the elite Fortune 500 or is a recently founded, and perhaps even financially strapped, small business. However, on-the-job training (OJT) is perhaps most critical in small to medium-sized organizations lacking the staff, the internal expertise, or the other resources to conduct planned training or maintain a cadre of training professionals. That is significant for at least one important reason: according to the Small Business Administration, organizations employing nineteen or fewer employees are the engines of job creation in the United States.

The stakes for improving on-the-job performance are increasingly high. Competitive conditions are global, and U.S. employers often find themselves outpriced by the lower labor and benefit costs in other nations. More effectively planned OJT is one way by which to individualize training, avoid one-size-fits-all approaches that ignore the nuances of individual needs, and ensure that organizations provide appropriate experiences so that individuals can build their competencies.

Why Improve OJT?

There are several important reasons for organizations to improve OJT. Each reason relates directly to the need for this book.

First, when OJT has been carefully planned, organizations can effectively reduce the unproductive breaking-in period of newcomers. Time is now critical as a strategic resource. Customers and competition alike mandate it. Newcomers must become fully productive as soon as possible so that they can take their place as fully functioning team members and share the work burden with others who may be feeling stressed out—as is often the case in downsized firms in which individuals must produce more than what was once expected of them. OJT is thus a competitive weapon to make workers "performance-ready" faster so they can keep pace with dynamic changes in their jobs. The rapid deployment capability of OJT is all the more appealing so that workers' skills are tapped "just-in-time" to meet organizational needs. That need is only intensified by the increasing use of short-term, contingent, flexitime, and flexiplace workers who must be made productive as quickly as possible if their temporary employers are to receive the greatest benefits from their efforts (Kenyon, 1999).

Second, planned OJT can relieve employee anxiety and reduce avoidable turnover. If left to learn jobs through "sink or swim" (unplanned) methods, employees may feel anxious about not knowing what they are expected to do, how they are expected to do it, or why they need to do it. If no organized effort is made to socialize them or introduce them to their job duties, they may become turnover statistics. Of course, most managers want to avoid turnover because it increases training costs and disrupts production. One classic, and often cited, research study suggested that training is a frequently overlooked—albeit important—factor in job satisfaction (Kovach & Cohen, 1992). Another classic, and often cited, research study revealed that women employees, at least, are more likely to remain with an employer that provides OJT than one providing off-the-job training (Lynch, 1991).

Third, planned OJT may provide early warning about employee basic skills problems. The United States continues to face a basic skills crisis that threatens the competitiveness of American industry in the global marketplace. While OJT is not the only way by which basic skills deficiencies can be surfaced or addressed, it may be integrated with basic skills training through the *functional job*

context approach to basic skills training, where the work functions themselves become the foundation for basic skills training. In such cases, the likelihood of success is magnified. Some employers have gone so far as to begin teaching basic
skills in the workplace (Bolch, 2002).

Fourth, planned OJT may lead employers to find better ways to address
individual learning disabilities. As a result of the Americans with Disabilities Act,
civil rights protection was extended to the disabled in organizations employing
more than twenty-five people. Employers are obliged to make *reasonable accommodation* for disabled individuals–including the estimated 3 to 16 percent of the
workforce experiencing learning disabilities. To that end, employers must have
some way to address such disabilities once identified and verified. OJT is a possible means to do that, though doing so may necessitate special training for on
the-job trainers.

Fifth, planned OJT may lead to high-quality customer service. Customers'
perceptions often result from *moments of truth* in which they come in contact with
an organization's employees (Albrecht & Zemke, 1985). Customers are more
often served by workers on the firing line than by supervisors, managers, or executives. That means a well-trained, more than a merely courteous, workforce
will be the best tool to ensure high-quality customer service. OJT is one means
by which to achieve that end.

Sixth, planned OJT may be a means by which to continuously improve
product or service quality. Total Quality guru W. Edwards Deming (1986) en-
shrined "instituting OJT" as one of his famous fourteen points for total quality,
and training figures prominently in ISO Quality Standards (Eline, 1998; *ISO
9000,* 1992; Von Hoffman, 1998). OJT can lead to the continuous improvement of product or service quality, thereby contributing to the goals of a total
quality initiative.

Employees have a vested interest in their own on-the-job learning (OJL) as
much as employers should have a vested interest in OJT. To remain employed
at a time when dramatic economic restructuring is tearing at the fabric of life in
the United States–and, indeed, in all nations–individuals have a stake in seeing
that they receive the best training possible. More than one authority has com-
mented on the growing importance of keeping employee skills current in a period of turbulent change. Workers must upgrade their knowledge and skills
consistantly to remain marketable. And OJT can be a good investment at a time
when organizations are cutting back traditional training (Gale, 2001).

Since 90 percent or more of an individual's learning occurs on the job (Watson, 1979), OJL has long been an important part of an individual's continued
marketability. When firms did not "downsize" and individuals did not "jump
ship" as often as in recent years, that continued marketability may have been less

important than it is now. But in the current economic climate, OJL is a powerful tool to help individuals find jobs, keep jobs, advance to other jobs, and move advantageously from one organization to others. Learning how to learn–an essential component of OJL–is a powerful hedge against skill obsolescence and prolonged unemployment, provided that what individuals learn can be transferred across organizations (Rothwell, 2002).

Purpose

This book is written for trainers, although many others–including supervisors, operating managers, and experienced employees–may benefit from it. A departure from other treatments of OJT that focus attention on one-on-one training methods only, this book is an action guide that describes how to establish and operate a comprehensive OJT program geared to all job categories in *one* organizational culture. Such a program, we believe, will improve employee performance and increase organizational profitability. This book can also be used to improve one-on-one OJT conducted by supervisors or co-workers and can thus serve as a reference guide for developing train-the-trainer experiences.

Overview of the Contents

A pretest opens the book. It should help employers assess the status of OJT in their organizations. It also serves as an advance organizer of the book's contents.

The book is organized into three parts and eleven chapters.

Part One consists of Chapters One through Four. It lays the foundations for the book by showing what is needed to build an effective organizational climate to support OJT.

Chapter One lays the book's foundation by explaining why OJT is important, briefly reviewing what has been written about it, listing major barriers to its effective use, and offering ideas for overcoming those barriers. Chapter Two offers guidance for establishing an OJT program; Chapter Three reviews key management issues that should be addressed during program start-up; and Chapter Four describes methods of training the trainers and learners for their roles in OJT and OJL.

Part Two consists of Chapters Five through Ten. It is based on DAPPER, a model for OJT and an acronym made up of the first letters of steps in the planned OJT process (See Figure I.1):

- *Di*scovering needs for planned OJT
- *A*nalyzing work, worker, and workplace for OJT
- *P*reparing planned OJT
- *P*resenting planned OJT
- *E*valuating the results of OJT
- *R*eviewing aids to planned OJT

Part Three consists of Chapter Eleven only. This part, and this final chapter, emphasizes six key lessons about successful planned OJT programs.

The book concludes with a glossary that defines key terms used throughout the book and a list of resources. Finally, a CD-ROM accompanies the book. It provides all worksheets appearing in the book and contains an entire train the trainer workshop on OJT, complete with reproducible slides, a participant workbook, and a leader's guide.

FIGURE I.1. THE DAPPER MODEL.

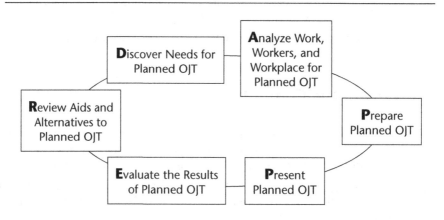

PRETEST

How to Assess Post-Training Job Performance

Complete the following pretest before you read this book. Use it as a diagnostic tool to help you assess the need for a planned OJT program in your organization. You may also use it as an advance organizer to refer you directly to topics in the book that are of special importance to you now.

The Pretest

Directions: Read each item in the pretest on the next page. Circle T (true), N/A (not applicable), or F (false) in the left column next to each item. Spend about 10 minutes on the pretest. Be honest! Think of OJT in your organization as you believe the learners see it–not necessarily as you think it is, as you hope it is, as you believe it will eventually become, or as you think that managers think it should be. When you finish, score and interpret the results using the instructions appearing at the end of the pretest. Then be prepared to share your responses with others in your organization as a starting point for improving OJT. If you would like to learn more about one item below, refer to the number in the right column to find the chapter in this book in which the subject is discussed.

Circle your response in the left-hand column for each response below.

Has your organization established each of the following for a planned OJT program:

T	N/A	F	1.	A written purpose statement?	2
T	N/A	F	2.	Written program goals?	2
T	N/A	F	3.	Written program objectives?	2
T	N/A	F	4.	Customers to be served by the program?	2
T	N/A	F	5.	A written program policy statement?	2
T	N/A	F	6.	A written program philosophy?	2
T	N/A	F	7.	A program action plan?	2
T	N/A	F	8.	A schedule of program events based on the action plan?	2
T	N/A	F	9.	Who will oversee the organization's program?	3
T	N/A	F	10.	Incentives/rewards for those who will conduct planned OJT?	3
T	N/A	F	11.	Incentives/rewards for those who receive planned OJT?	3
T	N/A	F	12.	A means to budget for planned OJT?	3
T	N/A	F	13.	A means to keep records for individuals participating in planned OJT?	3
T	N/A	F	14.	Training workshops for on-the-job trainers in support of program goals?	4
T	N/A	F	15.	Training workshops for on-the-job learners in support of program goals?	4
T	N/A	F	16.	A means for discovering needs for planned OJT?	5
T	N/A	F	17.	A means to analyze work, worker, and workplace?	6
T	N/A	F	18.	A means by which to prepare planned OJT?	7
T	N/A	F	19.	A means to present planned OJT?	8
T	N/A	F	20.	A means to evaluate the results of planned OJT?	9
T	N/A	F	21.	Procedures for selecting alternatives to, or supplements for, planned OJT?	10

Scoring and Interpreting the Pretest

Give your organization *1 point for each T* and a *0 for each F or N/A*. Total the number of Ts and place the sum in the line next to the word TOTAL.

Total: _____

Then interpret your score as follows:

19 or more	Your organization is apparently using effective OJT practices. While improvements can be made, the critical success factors for a planned OJT program are already in place—assuming, of course, that you answered the Pretest honestly and that the score does not merely represent wishful thinking.
15 to 18	Improvements could be made to OJT practices. On the whole, however, the organization is proceeding on the right track.
12 to 14	OJT practices in your organization do not appear to be as effective as they should be. Significant improvements should be made.
11 or less	OJT practices are ineffective in your organization. They are probably a source of costly mistakes, productivity losses, and unnecessary employee turnover. Take immediate corrective action.

PART ONE

FOUNDATIONS OF OJT

B uilding an Effective Organizational Climate to Support OJT

CHAPTER ONE

THE BENEFITS OF EFFECTIVE ON-THE-JOB TRAINING

On-the-job training (OJT) may be *planned* (structured) or *unplanned* (unstructured) (see the Glossary for formal definitions of basic terms in this book). When most people think of OJT, they are thinking of unplanned training. As Filipczak (1993, p. 30) explains, "OJT has often meant having a new employee 'go sit by Nellie' or follow Sam around the factory floor playing monkey-see, monkey-do." It is the ubiquitousness of unplanned OJT that prompted Evans and Herr (1978, p. 10) in their classic book to write that "OJT has always been relatively haphazard. The new worker observes, practices, learns by trial and error, and occasionally receives direct instruction (if the experienced worker does not feel threatened by the competition)." And as Lester Thurow (1992, p. 275) pointed out, "'Following Joe around,' the American system of on-the-job training, simply isn't a system." However, owing to the blinding speed with which new innovations must be applied in the workplace, the traditional and unplanned approach to on-the-job training is yielding to a planned approach that is on the cutting edge of training practice and is closely allied to recent research on workplace learning. Planned OJT may be moving to center stage as an effective tool to create learning organizations (Dobson & Tosh, 1998; Senge, 1990).

But what is planned OJT? Why is it important? What are the major barriers to its use? And how may those barriers be surmounted? This chapter answers these questions and, in doing so, lays the foundation for this book. We begin with a case study that dramatizes key issues associated with OJT.

Unplanned OJT: A Case Study

Harriett Endover is upset. After three weeks as a desk clerk on the midnight to 8 a.m. shift at a hotel, she still does not know what she is expected to do. A college student working part-time, she is nervous about being ill-prepared to do her new job. Harriett was elated when she first received the job offer. She was convinced the job would be perfect for a student. As the interviewer explained it, Harriet would have little to do because most hotel guests would be asleep during her shift. After one hour of paperwork each night, she would be allowed time to study. After Harriett eagerly accepted the job, her interviewer told her to report to night supervisor Barton Kent. Her training would occur on the job.

On her first night, Harriett found Barton to be very amiable. He treated her in a dignified and courteous way, and she felt instantly at ease with him. However, as the days wore on, Harriett drew a sharp distinction between Barton the supervisor and Barton the trainer. Barton the supervisor could be inspiring. He was a zealot about the hospitality industry and could expound on its virtues for hours. Harriett was impressed with his ability to wax philosophic about what was to her a pedestrian subject. At one point, he confided to her that his life's goal was to manage a large hotel in a major city. However, Barton the trainer was not effective. Although Harriett asked him numerous questions about the hotel chain and the business practices of this particular hotel, she did not receive clear answers. Nor did she receive organized training on her work duties; rather, she was expected to shadow Barton as he dealt with minute work details. He did not instruct her on how to handle fires, room burglaries, medical emergencies, or other major problems that might arise on the night shift. Harriett felt uncomfortable because she was ill-equipped to deal with major problems she felt that she might encounter on the job. She was convinced she knew just enough to be dangerous. In her opinion, her OJT was a waste, and she interpreted that as a sign that this hotel was poorly managed. She told her friends:

> I find this situation intolerable. Although I like Barton, he just does not seem capable of structuring information in a way that I can absorb. He handles work problems as they come up, leaving it to me to figure out what I don't know, and he doesn't have time to answer my questions since he's so busy doing the work I should be doing. I don't fault him. The hotel should have furnished him with a training plan for new desk clerks. Since the company has not done so, I assume it is not well-managed. I must admit that, given what he has told me about the recent history of the night desk at this hotel, it is unlikely I will face many difficult-to-handle situations. Still, I don't feel at ease when I am so helpless and unproductive. At the rate I'm being trained, it will take months for me

to function on my own in what is really a simple job, and I have received such disorganized training that it's difficult for me to organize what I learn.

Then Harriett announced to her friends that she had decided to quit the job and would give her notice the next day.

At the same time, Barton gave Harriett's employment interviewer this report:

Harriett is doing fine. I just wish I could give her more organized training. I do not have time to do that. If I did, I would probably start out by preparing a detailed job description that sets forth the essential job functions of a night desk clerk. I would then use the job description to develop a training plan, which I would write down so I would not forget anything, and I would develop a training schedule to clarify when she would be trained on each essential job function. In all likelihood, I would begin the training by instructing her in exceptions to normal routine—such as fires, burglaries, vandalism, and lost keys—and then move to routine job functions. For each function, I would explain what she should do; how, when, why, and where she should do it; and how her performance will be evaluated. When she finished that training, she would be certified and released from further dependence on a trainer. Her training would also include attending a classroom orientation conducted by the Human Resource Department, and I would ask one of her experienced co-workers to serve as a mentor to help her get to know the people with whom she will be working. As it is, however, I feel that I am wasting time having her just watch me as I do the work that she will eventually be expected to do. I'm not sure whether she will be able to do it when she has to. Also, there is no organizational scheme to what she is learning; instead, her training is organized by the chaotic, momentary work demands that I am facing. That must translate into wasted salary for us both.

In my opinion, all new desk clerks should have planned training in essential job functions, and other functions should be covered depending on the shift to which they are assigned. We should devise an on-the-job training plan and schedule for new desk clerks on each shift. The plan and schedule could be modified, as necessary, to take each individual's work experience into account.

Importance of OJT

As the preceding case study illustrates, in its most elementary form, OJT is simply *job instruction occurring in the work setting and during the work*. Harriett received unplanned OJT, though her supervisor was keenly aware that planned OJT would be preferable. Unplanned OJT is not organized according to the job performance needs of the intended learner; rather, it is driven by work demands and crises. That approach prolongs the training period unnecessarily and can evoke anxiety and even a decision to quit, as happened in Harriet's experience. In contrast, planned OJT centers around what the learner needs to know and do to perform the job, why these activities are important, and what work results should be obtained.

As the case study also dramatizes, there are good reasons to pay attention to OJT. And OJT, as well as topics closely associated with it, has been a frequent topic for publication in recent years (see Hodges, 2001; Jacobs, 2003; Lawson, 1997; Pike, Solem, & Arch, 2000; Walter, 2001). According to a 1995 study conducted by the U.S. Bureau of Labor Statistics, which was one of the largest studies done of training in the United States, OJT expenditures reached about $48.4 billion in 1995 and about 96 percent of all employees participating in the study had received some informal training of the kind represented by OJT (Benson, 1997). Low-skilled and less-educated workers in the United Kingdom expressed a desire for more OJT in a recent study (Cannell, 2002), and OJT was found to be the most common form of training in the U.K. (Cannell, 1999). A study conducted in the United States revealed that 62 percent of what people learn about their work in manufacturing firms comes from informal methods such as OJT (Verespej, 1998).

Salary expenses, particularly those linked to one-on-one training, can represent a sizable investment for organizations. The precise size of this investment is suggested by the results of a classic 1989 research study that revealed that, during their first three months of employment, new employees spend approximately 30 percent of their time in OJT (Barron, Black, & Loewenstein, 1989). Some employers—such as small business—may even value OJT more than they do formal training (Blackburn & Hankinson, 1989). Individuals have a stake in OJT as well, since a survey of 995 heads of households demonstrated a link between training received and wage growth (Brown, 1989). Additional investments typically made as newcomers receive OJT include the cost of lost production from experienced workers who are assigned to help newcomers learn the ropes and the cost of increased scrap rates if newcomers make costly mistakes while participating in OJT (Evans & Herr, 1978).

The quality of an organization's OJT directly impacts how long it takes to train newcomers, how much turnover the organization experiences (Prickett, 1997b; Winkler & Janger, 1998), how well non-English-speaking immigrants can be accommodated in the U.S. workplace ("United Nations," 1998), how women progress in their careers (McDonald & Hite, 1999), how quickly workers can be retrained to meet swiftly changing workplace demands, how satisfied workers feel about their jobs and working conditions, how workers perceive organizational management, how well-equipped workers are to make quality products or offer quality service, how well the organization manages the transfer of knowledge from one generation of workers to their successors (Lahti, 2002), how satisfied workers are in their teams (Williams, 1998), and how well-prepared workers are to adapt to new technology. Expatriate success is dependent on the mentoring—a topic closely related to OJT—they receive (Feldman & Bolino, 1999). A Sears study found that a 5 percent improvement in employee satisfaction can lead to a 1.3 percent increase in customer satisfaction and that worker training provided on the job can be an important factor in improving employee satisfaction (Kiger, 2002).

Many companies have experienced major benefits from planned OJT; examples include Boeing, SGS Tool Company, and Norton Manufacturing (Barron, 1997; "Case Study: OJT in Action," 1994; "Case Study: Tutoring," 1995). Although there has been much bias toward e-learning in recent years, some observers advise trainers to adopt OJT approaches to e-learning (Malcolm, 2001). OJT has also been advised as a strategy to be used with high-turnover workers, such as temps and contingent employees (Walter, 1999) and has been shown to be important in sales training (Rothwell, Donahue, & Park, 2002), technical training (Rothwell & Benkowski, 2002), and leadership training (Rothwell & Kazanas, 1999).

Coaching, Mentoring, and OJT

Coaching is a term closely related to OJT. It is interesting that, with workers below supervisor, the term OJT is usually used. With professional, technical, supervisory, management, or executive workers, a preferred term is often coaching, which can be synonymous with OJT. Coaching can also be unplanned or planned. It can even be offered online (Barbian, 2002b; Feldman, 2002; Patton, 2001). Some suggest that it is not only used to help people learn what to do and how to do it but, in some cases, is becoming a perk (Bolch, 2001). It can be a strategy to help average performing managers learn from exemplars (Brown, 2000), and it can also be a strategy to help turn around problem performers (Donaldson & Folb, 1999). Some even recommend it for stress reduction (Conlin, 1999). Demand for executive coaches increased 1,000 percent in one year (Filipczak, 1998). Much has been written about coaching in recent years. See, for instance, Berglas (2002), David (2002), Davidson (2002), Homan and Miller (2002), Prost (2000), and Smith and Sandstrom (1999). A key element in the success of coaching, as for OJT, is management commitment (Ellinger, 1999).

Mentoring is, of course, also related to OJT—and enjoys a long history (Benabou & Benabou, 2000; Kaye & Scheef, 2000; Latemore & Callan, 1998). Mentors are simply teachers, and mentees are simply learners. Mentoring may imply less formality or structure than OJT, but it can also be critically important. Often, mentors offer advice on anything—ranging from what to do and how to do it to how to cope with life problems or organizational politics. One research study found, for instance, that those with mentors earned between $5,000 and $22,000 more per year than those who did not have the benefit of mentors (Tyler, 1998). Much has been written about mentoring (Berube, 1996; Dockery & Sahl, 1998; "Mentoring Takes Off," 1996; Wachtel & Veale, 1998; Warner, 2002). Excellent materials are available to support a mentoring program that, while written for use in schools, can be easily adapted to other organizational settings (Bidwell, 1997a, 1997b; Morrow & Fredin, 1999).

A Short History of Planned OJT

As planned OJT is understood today, it emerged as a result of U.S. wartime needs early in the twentieth century. During World War I, Charles R. (Skipper) Allen introduced a method of training shipbuilders that led to the first distinction between planned and unplanned OJT. Basing his approach to OJT on the ideas of the nineteenth-century German psychologist Johann Friedrich Herbart, Allen suggested that trainers go through the following four steps and accompanying actions to improve training efficiency (McCord, 1987, p. 366, used with permission):

Step	*Action*
Preparation	Show: demonstrate to learners what they should do.
Presentation	Tell: explain to learners what they should do and why they should do it.
Application	Do: allow learners to try out the work.
Inspection	Check: follow up with the learners, providing praise for what they do right and specific feedback about what they should do to improve.

Taking his cues from Frederick W. Taylor and others who stressed industrial efficiency, Allen believed that the proper focus of OJT should be the *job* rather than the *individual*. Workers should be selected based on job demands and then trained to carry out the specific tasks they were hired to perform. Any training should be preceded by a job breakdown to clarify what the learners should do. OJT, Allen believed, should be carried out by supervisors so job incumbents could be held directly accountable for what they learned.

During World War II, Allen's simple four-step formula for on-the-job training was expanded to seven steps (McCord, 1987, p. 368, used with permission):

1. Show learners how to perform the task.
2. Review key points.
3. Allow learners to watch the instructor/supervisor perform the task a second time.
4. Allow learners to perform the simple parts of the job.
5. Guide learners to perform the whole job.
6. Let learners perform the whole job, but monitor their performance.
7. Release learners from training and allow them to perform on their own.

These seven classic steps came to be called *job instruction training* (JIT), after the government wartime program of the same name. Training based on these steps, it was discovered, resulted in increased production in the wartime industries, and these steps still work efficiently and effectively in today's industries. One possible reason for their enduring usefulness is that, taken together, they may effectively tap all four learning styles identified by Kolb (1984).

In recent years, however, OJT has been largely neglected. We see three major reasons for that. First, "Recent advances in the use of instructional technology have overshadowed OJT as a training method" (Jacobs & McGiffin, 1987, pp. 81–82). U.S. executives and managers seem more enamored with flashy, expensive, and technologically based training methods than they are with OJT. Moreover, managers have an expectation—seldom spoken but felt by training professionals nevertheless—that employer-based training should resemble formal schooling. Second, OJT has long been taken for granted. Employees and employers alike assume it will just happen—and, of course, usually it does. But the important question is, *How efficiently and effectively does it happen?* Third, OJT is often difficult to distinguish from the work itself. In the workplace, training, learning, and performing are often inextricably intertwined. Without a road map, managers find it difficult to tell when training is happening or when it should be happening.

Research on Planned OJT

Much organized research has been published on planned OJT. We searched many databases using many descriptors related to planned OJT and found many accounts of research on the subject. These accounts included case studies (for example, Al-Ali, 1996; Churchill & Burzynski, 1991; Harrison, 1994; Jacobs, 2002; Jacobs & McGiffin, 1987; "OJT in Japan," 2000; Sullivan & Miklas, 1985); survey results on training individuals about OJT (Rothwell & Kazanas, 1990b, 1990c, & 1990d; Rothwell, 2003); and studies comparing the relative costs and benefits of OJT to off-the-job training (Cullen, Sawzin, Sisson, & Swanson, 1976, 1978; Kovach & Cohen, 1992).

What has been published supports our view of the high value of planned OJT. For example, Jacobs and McGiffin (1987, p. 9) conducted a field study in "a large company that processes and packages a wide range of edible oils," focusing their research on the Lab Tech III position, which was filled by "entry-level, salaried employees." At the beginning of the study, new Lab Tech IIIs entered their jobs with minimal knowledge of work tasks and received an average of twelve weeks of unplanned OJT from their supervisors. The supervisors had not been trained to use planned OJT, and employee accountability had not been established through measurable job performance standards. Turnover in the job averaged five out of eighteen people annually. During their field work, Jacobs and McGiffin introduced three major changes: they trained supervisors on planned OJT; they analyzed the Lab Tech III job and devised a training manual suitable for self-instruction on the job; and they developed checklists (job aids) to help workers carry out their tasks and assess their own performance and progress. Jacobs and McGiffin's changes produced dramatic results. Training time was slashed from twelve to three weeks. Cost savings (computed by multiplying the value of reduced training time by the number of workers turning over each year, minus the project's cost) amounted to $10,000 in the first year.

Other case studies, although often anecdotal in kind and examining industrial rather than business, service, or governmental settings, demonstrate equally dramatic results from planned OJT. As reported by Marsh and Pigott (1992), for example, the Westvaco paper mill in Charleston, South Carolina, achieved significant cost savings by instituting a program in which equipment operators were able to learn through a combination of on-the-job presentations, demonstrations, and practice sessions. Scribner and Sachs (1990) compared planned and unplanned OJT in a factory stockroom and found real differences, with planned OJT more cost efficient and effective. Jacobs, Jones, and Neil (1992) compared planned and unplanned OJT in a truck assembly plant and found that planned OJT enjoyed distinct financial advantages. Mullaney and Trask (1992) reported on an effective five-step model that helps subject-matter experts conduct OJT at the Los Alamos National Laboratory. Subaru-Isuzu made use of a planned OJT program for its workers and experienced significant success with it (Martin, 1991). Cannell (1997) examined best practices in OJT, focusing his attention on Ryder, the Royal Air Force, British Aerospace, and McDonald's. Organizations have even employed professional ethnographers to determine what people really do on their jobs so that such knowledge can be transferred to others (Raimy, 2000)— new hires and potential successors.

Barriers to OJT

The barriers that impede organizations from establishing and conducting planned OJT can include key stakeholders who lack awareness of the differences between planned and unplanned OJT, who are unwilling to invest the effort required for planned OJT, and/or who claim there is insufficient time to carry it out. In addition, an organization can lack the necessary expertise to design or implement planned OJT. Levine (1996) has pinpointed five common myths about OJT—that it is free, that OJT coincides with production, that OJT is part of the job, that OJT lasts forever, and that OJT can be conducted by anyone—which, when debunked, can also serve as barriers to implementing effective OJT.

When an organization's key stakeholders, both in management and in unions, lack awareness, seeing no difference between planned and unplanned OJT, then they also see no other way to train people than by asking newcomers to shadow more experienced workers (the learning-by-osmosis method) or to jump in and perform the work without training (the sink-or-swim method). This barrier is probably more common than most people care to admit.

The key stakeholders who lack willingness are also content to permit OJT to occur through learning-by-osmosis or sink-or-swim methods. Some of them feel that they had to learn from the school of hard knocks so others must pay their dues and learn the same way. Other stakeholders feel that workers thrust into a job without any preparation will gain stamina. However, whatever the superficial appeal of these rationalizations, they can also result in an increase in avoidable turnover of otherwise good workers, a loss of customer goodwill, more rework due to defective production, and a heightened sense among employees that management does not care—or does not know how poorly it is managing.

Lack of time is a common excuse for not planning OJT. In downsized organizations, for instance, both workers and supervisors are shouldering more duties than they have historically had to handle. When individuals are stressed out from juggling their traditional job functions along with additional work that they have not performed previously, planning and carrying out OJT ranks as a low priority, taking a back seat to fighting daily fires and getting the work out. Unfortunately, once again, there is a price to be paid for not devoting time to OJT: new hires, who could provide much-needed assistance to overworked people, are not as quickly utilized as they could be because their training is deficient or prolonged. Indeed, new hires faced with unplanned on-the-job training may grow disenchanted with what they see or may feel anxious about their inability to help those who are overworked. Some workers may quit as a result. Their departure will only intensify morale problems among downsizing's survivors or among employees in high-pressure work environments.

In organizations that lack expertise, having no in-house ability to carry out job breakdowns, establish training plans and schedules, implement those plans through structured work experiences, and evaluate results, it is common to find subject-matter experts who have no knowledge of instructional design left to their own devices to establish and carry out OJT for new workers. Lack of OJT expertise is common in small businesses, which typically have no training departments, and in large organizations when the training department is downsized or is not partnering with operating departments to offer instruction on OJT methods or to design and deliver planned OJT.

Surmounting Barriers to OJT

How can organizations surmount these barriers to planned OJT? While the answers to that question depend somewhat on each organization's culture, we can offer some general advice.

Key members of organizations' management—and union officials, when appropriate—must overcome their lack of awareness and learn the difference between planned and unplanned OJT (Ferman, Hoyman, Cutcher-Gershenfeld, & Savoie, 1991). Often, this change in attitude, knowledge, and procedure will require a change champion, an early innovator within the organization who identifies the need for organizational change and advocates it to others. In this instance, the change champion would begin by collecting information about differences between planned and unplanned OJT. Another way to promote the change to awareness is to benchmark, comparing OJT practices in well-known or local organizations inside and outside one's industry to one's current practices (Younger, 1994). Yet another way to begin this change is for stakeholders to ask supervisors and employees how they feel OJT could be improved, since poor OJT is a common complaint among newcomers and supervisors alike. Their suggestions can then guide the search for ways to improve OJT on a continuous basis.

To overcome their lack of willingness, an organization's stakeholders must be convinced that a change from unplanned to planned OJT is worthwhile. At a minimum, change champions must address such questions as these: What measurable cost savings, if any, will result from planned OJT? What will the organization gain by sponsoring planned OJT? More specifically, what is the evidence that planned OJT will reduce operating costs, slash avoidable turnover, increase quality, improve customer service, improve employee morale, and/or achieve other goals prized by the organization and its key decision makers or stakeholders? What health, safety, and legal compliance problems may be solved, or even averted, by using planned OJT? The change champion must also be willing to do some personal selling to convince those favoring unplanned OJT about its disadvantages.

To overcome individuals' lack of time, the organization must make planned OJT a priority, establishing a policy of emphasizing the importance of OJT, for example, or examining the resources, incentives, and rewards provided for OJT and increasing them as appropriate.

To overcome lack of expertise, the organization may need to sponsor at least one person to become expert in planned OJT. This step may require sending that person to outside training about OJT, encouraging managers' and workers' reading on the topic, offering in-house training on planned OJT through commercially available do-it-yourself training packages, tapping in-house training professionals to offer consulting help, or engaging external consultants who specialize in planned OJT. While taking all these steps to remove your organization's barriers to planned OJT is often easier said than done, these steps must be taken if a planned OJT program is to enjoy any chance of success.

Summary

In this chapter we defined planned OJT, explained why it is important, distinguished it from mentoring and coaching, provided a brief history of planned OJT, summarized important research about OJT, identified possible barriers to its use, and supplied ideas on how to surmount those barriers. In the next chapter we offer advice about how to begin organizing a planned OJT program for an organization.

CHAPTER TWO

BUILDING THE RIGHT FOUNDATION

From Identifying Goals to Establishing an Action Plan

To function across job categories, locations, and work groups, an OJT program must be *organized*–that is, it must be thoughtfully established to achieve its intended purposes. (From this point on, "OJT program" will always refer to a *planned* OJT program.) These purposes, in turn, should be driven by issues important to the organization. In this chapter, you will learn how to establish an OJT program according to the following model:

1. Determine the OJT program's purpose(s).
2. Clarify program goals and objectives.
3. Identify program customers.
4. Formulate program policy and philosophy.
5. Develop a program action plan and schedule.

By addressing the issues in the model, you will take the first important steps in OJT program development.

Determine the OJT Program's Purpose

Different organizational decision makers will have differing expectations of an OJT program. It is thus unlikely that the program will serve only one purpose. Nevertheless, establishing common program expectations and priorities is important, and that is the point of determining *program purpose.* An OJT program should have an explicit statement of purpose. The more clearly that purpose is communicated to all stakeholders, the easier it will be to chart program direction across the organization and hold leaders and participants accountable for results.

Questions to Ask

To clarify program purpose, decision makers should initially focus on one major question: *What is the chief result intended from the program?* Armed with the answer(s) to that question, program leaders and participants should be better equipped to realize that purpose. The purpose statement of an OJT program should also answer these more detailed questions:

- What learning needs should the program meet?
- Who are the targeted participants?
- When should targeted participants be served?
- Where should targeted participants be served?
- Why should targeted participants be served in this way?
- How should the OJT program be integrated with employee orientation, off-the-job training, near-the-job training, off-site education, cross-training, or other organizationally sponsored learning activities?
- How should the OJT program be integrated with workforce planning, recruitment, selection, compensation, employee benefits, work design, organizational design, and labor relations?
- How should the OJT program be integrated with the organization's strategic plan?
- How should newcomers be introduced to the organization, an organizational unit, a job, or a work function?
- How should the organization make newcomers feel welcome?
- How should the organization expose newcomers to effective, positive role models?

Information to Gather

Information about program purpose can be gathered from four main sources.

Experienced Program Participants. Past program participants or experienced job incumbents should have benefitted from OJT and thus be able to answer such questions as these:

- How were you oriented and trained on the work you do?
- What OJT methods do you feel are especially effective or ineffective based on your own orientation or OJT experiences?

- What have you learned about your work through experience that you wish you had been trained in earlier?
- How were you introduced to the organization, organizational unit, work, or work task?
- How do you feel newcomers should be welcomed to a new work setting and helped to fit in?
- How can employees' self-esteem be reinforced during OJT?
- Who are the positive, effective role models to whom newcomers should be exposed?
- How should newcomers be advised to manage any negative role models whom they may encounter?
- How much responsibility for OJT do you believe should be shouldered by each of these groups: learners, trainers, supervisors, and the organization?

Past participants in OJT may also be asked for information about critical incidents in their OJT experiences that shaped their opinions. What specific incidents during their employment with the organization can they describe as especially illustrative of what to do in OJT? Answers to that question can both define the parameters and clarify the desirable purpose(s) of an OJT program.

Present Program Participants. Present participants in OJT and inexperienced job incumbents also have opinions about OJT and a personal stake in it. Their opinions are worth knowing if training is to be effective. While they may not be knowledgeable about what they should learn, they may be quite knowledgeable about how they can most effectively learn. They should thus be consulted for answers to such questions as the following:

- How do you learn best? Reflect on past situations in which you were asked to learn, and determine what methods worked best for you.
- What do you feel are especially effective and ineffective OJT methods? How do you account for your opinions?
- What problems, if any, are you already encountering that are intensified because you did not receive adequate OJT?
- How do you feel about your on-the-job trainers? Why do you feel as you do?
- How do you feel about the match between what you are learning in OJT and what you are seeing others do?
- How convinced are you that a systematic plan and schedule guides your training? Or do you feel that OJT is just fitted in haphazardly somehow during your daily work?
- How are you being made to feel welcome, and how are the trainers reinforcing your self-esteem?

- Do you feel you are seeing positive, effective role models?
- In your opinion, what are your responsibilities in OJT? What are the responsibilities of your trainer, your supervisor, and the organization?

Supervisors. Supervisors of past and present OJT participants are potential sources of information about program purpose. They can be asked these questions:

- How would you define the desirable purpose(s) of an OJT program?
- How well do you feel OJT has been planned and carried out in the past, and how is it being done now?
- What specific incidents can you point to that illustrate especially good or bad OJT methods or results?
- How do you feel OJT should be handled, and why?
- What do you perceive to be the responsibilities of yourself, learners, learners' co-workers, and others in OJT?

Customers. Customers have their own perspective on OJT, based on the results OJT achieves. These perceptions are worthy of note even though customers are not often positioned to make firsthand observations about OJT. Customers can be asked such questions as these:

- Judging from your experiences with our employees, what did they do or not do that you found especially good or bad? (Describe a situation in which you were personally involved to illustrate your point.)
- What training would you recommend, and why?
- What pleases you most and least about the service you have received from this organization?

The purpose of an OJT program can be surmised from the various stakeholders' answers.

Clarify Program Goals and Objectives

Program goals are the general results to be achieved. Goals are embedded in purpose statements. Rarely do they lend themselves to measurement or time-based tracking as program objectives do. Program goals for OJT might include:

- Slashing the length of unproductive breaking-in periods for newly hired, transferred, or promoted employees.
- Reducing reliance on sink-or-swim methods.

- Ensuring that learners receive work-related on-site instruction that is planned, scheduled, logically organized, and centered on meeting learners' needs.
- Increasing trainee and trainer accountability by clarifying precisely what OJT individuals received.
- Improving the match between the results people are supposed to achieve from their work and training plans and schedules that indicate how well individuals are prepared to perform their work efficiently and effectively.

These general direction-setting goals should be modified and prioritized so they address the pressing issues affecting your organization.

Program objectives stem from program goals. They answer such questions as these. How can achievement of the goal be measured? and What can be achieved over a specified time? Establish program objectives directly from program goals. Use an identifiable time horizon. Then state in writing the measurable program results that are to be achieved for each prioritized goal.

Identify Program Customers

To be successful, an OJT program must meet or exceed customer expectations. But who are these customers and what do they expect? OJT customers can be found in any organizational group. They may be categorized by level (executives, middle managers, supervisors, professionals, technical personnel, clerical personnel, skilled labor, and unskilled labor), by function (purpose within the organization), or by relationship to the OJT program (learners, trainers, or learners' organizational supervisors). Indeed, OJT programs may also be designed to meet the learning needs of groups external to the organization—including suppliers, distributing wholesalers, retailers, or other groups.

However customer categories are defined, customer expectations of an OJT program are sure to differ depending on customers' individual needs. Thus, the following three customer-related questions should be considered at the outset of program development:

- What groups are to be served?
- What are their expectations?
- What priorities can be established?

What Groups Are to Be Served?

Decide who will receive OJT. While the ultimate aim may be to offer OJT to all employees, that may not be possible upon program inception. Accordingly, choose a target group, the category of people whose training is likely to benefit the organization most. Starting with that group will make an impact on the organization and provide future leverage and credibility to the OJT program. Possible groups to target include employees selected by job category or occupation, experience level, or special needs.

What Are Customers' Expectations?

Do some brainstorming. Talk to members of the initial targeted group. Try to assess what they think about OJT. Do they have preconceived notions? Are they willing to listen to alternatives to "the way we've always done it"? How has OJT been handled with that group in the past? Write out the answers you find to these questions and then circulate them to group members and their immediate supervisors for comment. Use the results of this activity to help you clarify group members' expectations so that you have a basis on which to judge what you must do to meet or exceed these expectations.

What Priorities Can Be Established?

Compare group expectations and desired objectives to the list of goals provided earlier in this chapter. Set priorities to establish the customer expectations that will be pursued.

Formulate Program Policy and Philosophy

Although few organizations have prepared a written policy and philosophy on OJT, there are sound reasons for doing so: first, to match program action with driving business issues or strategic plans; second, to establish a foundation for consistency in OJT activities; and third, to communicate responsibilities throughout the organization.

What should be included in a written policy and philosophy statement for an OJT program? The appropriate answer to that question depends on the competitive forces affecting the organization and on the program purpose, goals, objectives, and customer expectations. The policy and philosophy statement should address, at length, all the key questions posed for a purpose statement.

To write a policy and philosophy for an OJT program, form an in-house advisory council. If possible, invite representatives from different job categories and locations and from different organizational levels and perspectives. The advisory council should be prepared to discuss issues affecting the organization and clarify how the OJT program can address those issues. By making the preparation of program policy and philosophy a council responsibility, you will build program ownership while also making it clear that the OJT program meets important organizational needs.

Develop a Program Action Plan and Schedule

While a policy and philosophy provides general program guidance, a *program action plan* provides detailed descriptions of the activities that should be performed to achieve the desired program purpose(s), goals, objectives, policy, and philosophy. Without a program action plan of who should do what, there will be no accountability for results.

A *program schedule* flows from the action plan and provides detailed information about what activities should be performed and when. For instance, a program action plan might describe new OJT roles for supervisors, co-workers, and prospective learners. The corresponding program schedule would then indicate when the organization will teach individuals their new roles by conducting train-the-trainer workshops on OJT and train-the-learner workshops on on-the-job learning.

Summary

In this chapter we provided advice on establishing a planned OJT program according to the following model:

1. Determine the OJT program's purpose(s).
2. Clarify program goals and objectives.
3. Identify program customers.
4. Formulate program policy and philosophy.
5. Develop a program action plan and schedule.

In the next chapter we offer advice on how to ensure the sound management and consistent results for a planned OJT program.

CHAPTER THREE

ENSURING SOUND MANAGEMENT AND CONSISTENT RESULTS

As an on-the-job training program is established, program management questions surface: Who should oversee the OJT program? What incentives or rewards should be offered to those who participate? How should the program be budgeted and funded? How should OJT records be kept? In this chapter we address the issues raised by these questions.

Oversight Responsibility

It is important to distinguish between responsibility for an *organization's OJT program* and for *one person's OJT.* Responsibility for one person's OJT is best regarded as shared by the trainer (a supervisor or experienced co-worker whose concern is the organization's productivity) and the learner (whose concern is his or her continued employability). Additionally, a union may have a stake in individuals' training.

Responsibility for the overall OJT program, however, should be fixed in one place. In that way, there will always be, in the words of the classic management theorist Henri Fayol (1930, p. 23), "one manager and one plan for all operations which have the same object in view." Accountability is thus ensured. But exactly who should bear the final responsibility? And why? These questions are fundamental to managing the OJT program. After all, it will be difficult to hold anyone accountable for program results if everybody—and therefore nobody—is responsible for it. What complicates the accountability issue is that responsibility for a program often leads to efforts to control it. Advice turns too easily into mandate. Yet to maintain widespread program ownership, continuous employee involvement at all levels is highly desirable. All those bearing responsibility for individual OJT should also have a say in decision making about program operations.

There are four possible places to affix final OJT program responsibility: with the organization's training professionals, its advisory councils, its line (that is, operating) managers, or work teams. Of course, these choices are correspondingly limited in organizations lacking a training function, an advisory council, or work teams. Also, no placement is ideal. There will be advantages and disadvantages no matter where final responsibility is placed.

Training professionals are well-positioned to accept program responsibility because their specialized knowledge of training should give them "expert power" (French & Raven, 1959, p. 163). More knowledgeable than most line managers about ways to facilitate adult learning, they are also uniquely positioned to ensure that effective integration is achieved among such related issues as selection, orientation, on-the-job training, off-the-job training, and other training, education, and development efforts. The potential disadvantages are that training professionals are often staff (advisory) specialists and are not on the firing line. They may thus not be in touch with daily OJT activities or challenges.

Advisory councils are well-positioned to accept program responsibility because they enjoy "referent power" (French & Raven, 1959, p. 161), the ability to link people, resources, and efforts. Depending on its membership, a council may wield considerable influence through the knowledge, authority, and ability represented by the members. However, organizations that choose this option should be alert for problems that arise because no one person is accountable for the program. Additionally, only some council members may be in touch with daily OJT activities.

Line managers have a vested interest in program success since they oversee the most employees. Members of this group possess expert knowledge about work processes and technology, although they may not be knowledgeable about efficient and effective methods for OJT. Moreover, they may have neither the time nor inclination to oversee OJT either for the organization or for their respective units. Thus, the problems to watch for if one line manager is made responsible for an organizationwide OJT program are the time the task consumes and the potential for turf battles with peers.

Work teams are also well-positioned to address OJT for their members. But problems can surface if team members lack the training in OJT methods, if they are too busy to manage them, or if they are unwilling to provide OJT.

Rewards and Incentives

Expectancy theory has been bolstered by a body of research evidence as an explanation of how people are motivated (Porter & Lawler, 1968; Vroom, 1964). Its precepts are consistent with intuition, too. Expectancy theory states that individuals exert effort when they see a need, believe success is realistically achievable, believe they will be rewarded for what they do, and value the reward they expect to achieve if successful. The same principles are applicable when organizations want to motivate people to take on an OJT program. It is therefore important that you review the rewards and incentives for OJT that both do and do not exist in your organization. This step should be performed no later than the start-up phase so that, if necessary, appropriate incentives and rewards can be established to support desired program results. Focus on trainers and learners when you consider incentives and rewards for OJT. For both groups, consider the following questions as they apply to your organization. Do members of each group:

- See a need for planned OJT?
- Believe OJT is realistically achievable?
- Believe they will be rewarded for participating in OJT?
- Value the reward(s) they expect to achieve if OJT is successful?

Take the time to answer these questions accurately, collecting information or posing the questions to your advisory council if necessary. Identify what incentives and rewards presently encourage trainers to conduct OJT and learners to participate in it. Then identify disincentives that may discourage trainers from conducting OJT or learners from participating in it. Examples of disincentives include lack of recognition for participating in OJT or the expectation that it can be conducted while trainers or learners maintain undiminished work output. Once you have answered the questions, use your answers as the basis for planning. Decide what you can realistically do to increase incentives and rewards or decrease disincentives.

Some interest has emerged over the last twenty years in alternative rewards and pay-for-skill programs as tools for encouraging practical learning and productivity improvement in the workplace. *Alternative rewards* are those that exist outside the traditional money-related motivators, such as wages, salaries, and employee benefits, already in place in most organizations. These alternative rewards include one-time bonuses for exceptional performance, special recognition, employee awards for outstanding achievement, and prized work assignments. Employees may be rewarded for their participation in OJT through any or all of these methods. Pay-for-skill programs, while still fraught with practical difficulties, are designed to compensate employees for what they learn. Often highly compatible with process improvement and team-based management, they are different from traditional compensation programs that reward individual output, group output, employee longevity, or individual merit. To establish a pay-for-skill program, an organization must take the following steps:

- Construct a hierarchy of essential job functions in the organization, division, department, or team.
- Identify the knowledge, skills, experience, education, and training linked to those functions that clearly equate to measurable productivity improvement.
- Establish training and cross-training plans to facilitate individual learning beyond the boundaries of traditional descriptions.
- Establish incentives or rewards for employees who achieve mastery or demonstrate competency in functions inside and outside those essential to their work.
- Provide OJT to help individuals achieve mastery in functions inside and outside those essential to their work.

Pay-for-skill programs encourage employees to learn new skills and build their competencies. They are thus ideally suited for bolstering OJT programs. They can also be instrumental in launching self-directed teams, since they encourage cross-training and can provide much-needed rewards during downsizings, in which retained workers must absorb more tasks while preserving production and quality. They also empower workers, making rewards within their own reach rather than something that is controlled by management.

However, pay-for-skill programs do have limitations. As these programs are implemented, workers may become confused about the true basis of incentives and rewards. Great care must therefore be taken during implementation to state the business needs driving the change in the reward and incentive policy and to clarify the differences between old and new compensation programs and how pay will now be determined. Also, although pay-for-skill programs can lead to a smaller cadre of highly skilled workers doing the same amount of work that a larger group of less skilled workers once did, some managers are reluctant to allow individuals to achieve greater rewards than they could realize through traditional pay programs. Nor do most employers want to pay employees for skills that are not immediately needed or to pay for learning that is not immediately recognizable as linked to measurable productivity improvement. To address these problems, some organizations arbitrarily limit the number of people who may participate in OJT or the number of knowledge-based promotions permitted. However, these limiting actions send a message to employees that conflicts with the message sent by a pay-for-skills program, and employees deduce that skill acquisition is less important than cost control. That message disheartens high achievers, who would otherwise pursue skill upgrading to realize greater rewards.

Budgeting and Funding

The budgeting and funding for OJT is rarely treated as a discrete activity. Instead, funding requirements for OJT are usually treated as an invisible expense of doing business, and that expense will usually be absorbed by operating departments during production. In most organizations, OJT will be neither budgeted for nor funded in the same way as formal group training, tuition reimbursement, or external vendors brought in to do training. Moreover, the expenses associated with OJT depend heavily on how often the organization replaces, transfers, promotes, demotes, and hires new workers or even on how it manages contingent workers or vendors.

One reason planned OJT has not commanded the attention it deserves is that most organizations do not possess adequate methods by which to track its costs or its benefits. However, it is possible to prepare such an estimate. Begin with an entry-level position that is frequently filled in your organization. List all the essential work functions on which newcomers to that position must be trained and, using information available in job evaluations or descriptions, estimate the monthly economic value of each activity. Then, using information supplied by operating managers, estimate how much time is needed to train a newcomer on each activity. Multiply the time required to train a newcomer on an activity by that activity's dollar value. After following the same procedure for all activities performed in that job category, estimate how many workers each year must be trained. This procedure will yield an estimate of OJT costs for the job category. Repeat the procedure for each commonly filled job category to arrive at a total dollar estimate for your organization's OJT expenses.

In most cases, the resulting estimate will be staggering, growing significantly when it is projected from one position to an entire organization. Under these circumstances, even small OJT improvements designed to cut training time can yield substantial savings, particularly in job categories experiencing the greatest turnover. Start with pilot OJT programs in one or more departments–targeting those with highest turnover first, since the greatest savings can often be realized in these locations. Then compare productivity before and after the programs are introduced, and use those figures to estimate program benefits. Then subtract the costs of program operations. If past research studies are any indication (Jacobs, Jones, & Neil, 1992; Jacobs & McGiffin, 1987), the results should demonstrate that OJT program benefits significantly outweigh costs.

Record Keeping

Record keeping is essential for a planned OJT program. It helps individuals remember what training they received, helps management document what training has been given, and helps protect the employer from litigation stemming
from charges of unfair employment discrimination or wrongful discharge. Without training records, an organization will lack an important source of information about training received in the past or desirable future training for
individuals—and will also lack information about the existing talent available in
the organization ("Skill Inventories," 2002). Moreover, it may be difficult to create a paper trail for pursuit of quality certification (ISO 9000, 1992).

Records should be kept in a way that is consistent with the organization's policies on establishing and documenting training plans and schedules. If, for example, each individual is given a training plan and schedule based on a current job
description, the plan itself could become a record if individual progress is noted
on it. If individualized development plans are the basis for OJT, then they too can
become records—so long as some effort is made to monitor and document individual progress. Records of OJT can answer such questions as the following:

- What kind of training did the learner receive (descriptive task title or essen-
  tial job function)?
- Who provided the training (name of trainer)?
- When was the training conducted (date and duration)?
- Where was it held (location)?
- How was it held (delivery methods)?
- Why was it held? How did it satisfy an individual need?
- How well did the individual perform in training? What were the results of
  training? Did the employee show evidence of competence? Did the employee
  satisfy minimum and measurable work performance standards?
- How was success in the training measured?
- How will future performance be measured? Were measurable job performance
  standards shared with the individual?
- What feedback was given about how well the individual performed? Was
  the individual coached to perform differently?
- What goals for future improvement were established?
- What coaching, if any, was offered to individuals about how they could im-
  prove performance?

Like written training plans or individual development plans, checklists also work well for record-keeping purposes because they can be signed by trainer and learner, indicating that both saw what was written. This information can also be placed in an individual's training or personnel file for future reference. In that way, both the learners and trainers can be held accountable for results.

Summary

In this chapter we offered advice on how to ensure the sound management and consistent results for a planned OJT program. In the next chapter we focus our attention on preparing trainers and learners for planned OJT by describing how they may be trained to carry out their roles in an organizationally sponsored planned OJT program.

CHAPTER FOUR

PREPARING TRAINERS AND LEARNERS

In this chapter we present the essential components of training workshops designed for those who conduct or receive planned OJT. In-house, train-the-trainer experiences are essential to the success of an OJT program. Without training on OJT, prospective trainers and learners may not know how to make the most of their workplace learning opportunities.

Training the Trainers

Relatively little is known about organizational practices in offering in-house, train-the-trainer experiences to workers or supervisors. One recent study, however, revealed that 77 percent of the leading companies in *Training* magazine's Top 100 Companies offer formal mentoring, 66 percent have job-shadowing programs, and job rotation is used by 51 percent of them (Barbian, 2002a). Most people learn about their work through informal mentors, hands-on experience, or work group support, but organizations continue to think of learning as synonymous with classroom-based or electronically-based training (Caudron, 2000).

A 1989 survey conducted by Rothwell and Kazanas (1990b, 1990c, and 1990d) shed some light on OJT practice. The methodology and results of that survey are summarized in this section so they can serve as benchmarking tools. Compare the survey results to practices in your organization. A comparable survey was conducted by Rothwell in 2003 to examine what has happened since the initial survey, and those results are presented later in the chapter.

To examine train-the-trainer practices, Rothwell and Kazanas drafted a four-part, twenty-item survey that asked for background information about respondents' organizations, the efforts of organizations that sponsor classroom training on OJT, the on-the-job learning in organizations that do not sponsor classroom training on OJT, and the tools and methods used to support OJT and the attitudes toward OJT. The survey was pretested with three seasoned training and development professionals, revised, and then mailed to a random sample of 500 members of the American Society for Training and Development in September 1989. The overall response rate was 26 percent. In all, fifty-two respondents claimed their organizations "presently offer in-house classroom training or 'train-the-trainer' programs on how to conduct OJT"; seventy-four respondents claimed their organizations do not offer such training; and two respondents did not answer the question. Large firms and manufacturers were more likely to offer such training than were small firms or nonmanufacturers.

The study also revealed that organizations offering classroom training about OJT have been doing so for some time. Of fifty-three respondents to part two of the survey, thirty (56.6 percent) indicated that their organizations have offered such training for four or more years. Twenty-eight respondents (53.8 percent) indicated that their classroom training on OJT is typically seven hours or longer. Others indicated fewer hours: five (9.6 percent) of the respondents said their classroom training was between one and two hours in length; seven (13.5 percent) said between three and four hours; five said between four and five hours; and another five said between five and six hours. The time devoted to training on OJT by organizations that conduct it indicates that they must view it as an activity with a substantial payoff. Topics treated in classroom training (see Table 4.1) match up well to the traditional models of OJT described in Chapter One. Survey respondents also indicated that immediate supervisors and co-workers perform most OJT, though full-time unit trainers also conduct a significant amount (see Figure 4.1.). Compared to respondents in organizations offering classroom training about OJT, respondents in organizations not offering that training were twice as likely to indicate that "top managers believe OJT is important but are not aware of how people can be trained to improve their methods of conducting OJT" (see Figure 4.2.).

TABLE 4.1. TOPICS TREATED IN EXISTING
CLASSROOM TRAINING ON OJT.

Topic	*Percentage of organizations treating the topic (N=52 respondents)*
Showing learners how to perform the task	96.2 percent
Having learners perform the task with the trainer observing	96.2 percent
Putting learners at ease	94.3 percent
Providing feedback to learners on how well they are performing a task or procedure	94.1 percent
Demonstrating all steps of effective OJT	92.3 percent
Emphasizing key points for learners to remember	90.6 percent
Analyzing work tasks or procedures	90.4 percent
Motivating learners to learn	90.4 percent
Telling learners how to perform a task	90.4 percent
Applying adult learning theory to OTJ	88.5 percent
Questioning learners on key points in what they are learning	88.5 percent
Clarifying the learners' performance standards	86.8 percent
Placing learners in the correct work setting to learn the task	86.5 percent
Showing learners how to correct errors they make	84.3 percent
Finding out what learners already know about the task	80.8 percent
Documenting training progress	79.6 percent
Modifying OTJ methods based on individual learning styles	65.4 percent
Modifying OTJ methods to deal with learning disabilities	52.0 percent

Source: Rothwell and Kazanas, 1990c, p. 21. Copyright 1990 by the Learning Systems Institute, 205 Dodd Hall, R-19, Florida State University, Tallahassee, FL 32306.

To find out what happened since the 1989 survey was conducted, Rothwell (2003) used the same survey in year 2003. The survey was pretested with three seasoned training and development professionals, revised, and then mailed to a random sample of 500 members of the International Society for Performance Improvement in March 2003. The overall response rate was 11.16 percent when the sample size was reduced to 475 because 25 questionnaires were returned as undeliverable. Most of the respondents' organizations represented a category of "other services" and employers of 5,000 workers or more. For graphic depictions of the survey respondents' demographics, see Figures 4.3 and 4.4.

FIGURE 4.1. WHO PERFORMS PLANNED OJT?

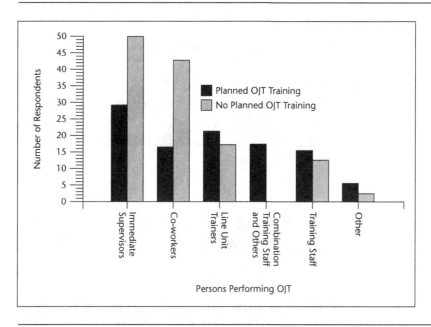

Source: Rothwell and Kazanas, 1990c, p. 21. Copyright 1990 by the Learning Systems Institute, 205 Dodd Hall, R-19, Florida State University, Tallahassee, FL 32306.

FIGURE 4.2. OPINIONS OF TOP MANAGERS ON OJT.

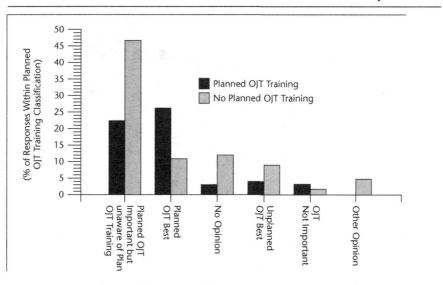

Source: Rothwell and Kazanas, 1990c, p. 21. Copyright 1990 by the Learning Systems Institute, 205 Dodd Hall, R-19, Florida State University, Tallahassee, FL 32306.

FIGURE 4.3. WHAT ARE THE INDUSTRY CATEGORIES OF SURVEY RESPONDENTS?

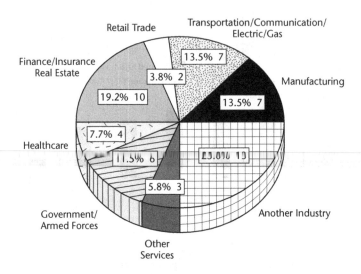

FIGURE 4.4. HOW MANY EMPLOYEES WORK IN YOUR ORGANIZATION?

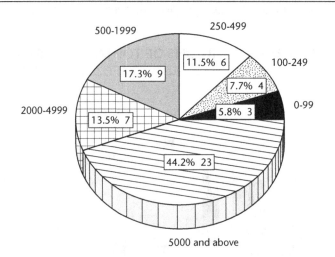

As in the 1989 study, the year 2003 study revealed that organizations offering classroom training about OJT have been doing so for some time. Of twenty-five respondents to part two of the survey, fourteen (68 percent) indicated that their organizations have offered such training for four or more years. Twelve respondents (63.15 percent) indicated that their classroom training on OJT is typically seven hours or longer. Topics treated in classroom training match up to the traditional models of OJT described in Chapter One (see Table 4.2). Survey respondents also indicated that immediate supervisors and and a combination of full-time in-house training staff and others perform most OJT, though full-time unit trainers also

TABLE 4.2. TOPICS ADDRESSED IN IN-HOUSE TRAIN-THE-TRAINER PROGRAMS FOR OJT.

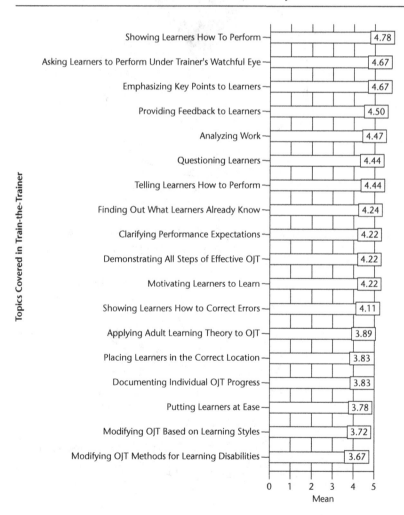

Topics Covered in Train-the-Trainer	Mean
Showing Learners How To Perform	4.78
Asking Learners to Perform Under Trainer's Watchful Eye	4.67
Emphasizing Key Points to Learners	4.67
Providing Feedback to Learners	4.50
Analyzing Work	4.47
Questioning Learners	4.44
Telling Learners How to Perform	4.44
Finding Out What Learners Already Know	4.24
Clarifying Performance Expectations	4.22
Demonstrating All Steps of Effective OJT	4.22
Motivating Learners to Learn	4.22
Showing Learners How to Correct Errors	4.11
Applying Adult Learning Theory to OJT	3.89
Placing Learners in the Correct Location	3.83
Documenting Individual OJT Progress	3.83
Putting Learners at Ease	3.78
Modifying OJT Based on Learning Styles	3.72
Modifying OJT Methods for Learning Disabilities	3.67

conduct a significant amount (see Figure 4.5). Twenty-one (41 percent) of the respondents in organizations not offering training agreed with the statement that "top managers believe that OJT is important but are not aware of how people can be trained to improve their methods of conducting OJT" (see Figure 4.6).

The material available on the CD-ROM included with this book provides a good starting point for preparing and delivering one or more in-house OJT workshops in your organization.

FIGURE 4.5. WHO CONDUCTS OJT?

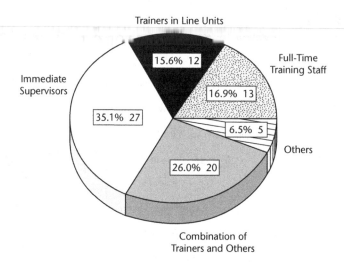

FIGURE 4.6. WHAT DO TOP MANAGERS BELIEVE ABOUT OJT IN YOUR ORGANIZATION?

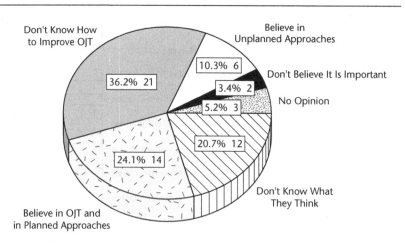

Training the Learners

Learners share responsibility for the success of OJT. With the advent of technology as a possible component of OJT, some observers have argued the need to build learner competence (Rothwell, 2002), since e-learning and other technologically driven or technologically assisted methods often place heavy reliance on learners' competencies and on organizational conditions that encourage real-time, on-the-job learning (see Martinez, 2002). Some might even argue that they bear the greatest responsibility for it because they should be self-directed and that getting learners to agree on what they need is sometimes the greatest challenge (Phillips, 1998). Workers should thus be encouraged to take responsibility for their own learning–and some companies have tried to enhance that through programs that encourage employee self-directedness (see Prickett, 1997a, 1997b). Our year 2003 survey results revealed that, when not given planned OJT, trainers believe that workers learn their jobs through other methods (see Figure 4.7).

But are learners self-directed? What training might enhance your learners' capabilities, thereby encouraging them to make the most of OJT opportunities offered to them?

FIGURE 4.7. HOW DO PEOPLE LEARN THEIR JOBS IF THEY DO NOT RECEIVE PLANNED OJT?

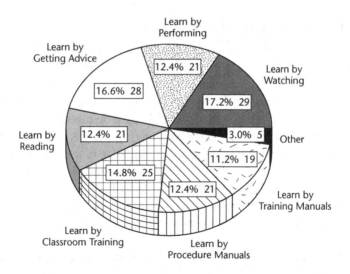

Are Learners Self-Directed?

Researchers have long debated learners' ability to be self-directed (see Merriam & Caffarella, 1991; Mezirow, 1985). Some researchers fervently believe that most adults are generally self-directed learners, noting that learning is not a solitary pursuit but requires the cooperation of others; others express doubts about learners' self-directedness (Brookfield, 1986); and still others accept learner self-directedness as a basic premise but place limitations on it. It could be that, as Aslanian and Brickell (1980) note in a classic work, adults are self-directed only when they face major life or work changes that motivate them to learn.

People must possess eight key characteristics if they are to pursue self-directed learning successfully. According to Guglielmino (1977), self-directed learners are open to learning, possess the self-concept that they are effective learners, are willing to take initiative and exercise independence in learning, accept responsibility for learning, love to learn, are capable of demonstrating creativity, possess a future orientation, and can apply basic study and problem-solving skills. Guglielmino's Self-Directed Learning Readiness Scale (SDLRS) is designed to assess an individual's readiness for self-directed learning (see Guglielmino & Guglielmino, 1988).

The management of organizations bears responsibility for ensuring that the right conditions exist to encourage individual self-directedness in learning. Concern about that has even prompted government officials in the U.K. to establish standards for organizational conditions that promote learning. Research has even revealed issues that help or hinder the learning climate (Rothwell, 2002).

Train-the-Learner Workshop Components

Valuable research has been performed on workplace learning (Marsick, 1987; Munnelly, 1987; Ravid, 1987; Rothwell, 2002; Rothwell, Sanders, & Soper, 1999; Skruber, 1987). Innovative training professionals are working to facilitate the changes in organizational environments that will make these environments more supportive of workplace learning and focused on meeting the needs of the whole person as well as unleashing the worker's knowledge, skills, and attitudes. These efforts, like planned OJT, are on the cutting edge of the learning and performance field, and they include numerous attempts to find ways to improve adults' skill at learning how to learn in the workplace. To improve the results of in-house OJT, therefore, it is worthwhile to train participants on how to improve their learning skills. Key components of in-house training for learners include:

- Learning to appreciate learning needs stemming from life, career, and job changes
- Identifying and making use of one's individual learning style
- Understanding the learner's role in learning

- Applying active listening skills
- Applying accelerated learning techniques
- Developing questioning skills

In the sections that follow, we elaborate on the workshop components we have just identified.

Learning Needs Stemming from Life, Career, and Job Changes. Occupational change in the United States is speeding up. That has prompted new interest in the age-old topic of life and career planning. The trend in business is to outsource work and use leased or temporary–even "use and throw away"–workers. The reasons behind this development include increases in governmental regulations, employee benefits costs, and corporate downsizing. Neither organizations nor individuals can take the employment relationship for granted any more. Workers must take more responsibility for their lives, careers, and job changes rather than assume, as many have done for so long, that other people will tell them what to do with their lives and careers and where to do it. To help themselves exercise this self-responsibility, workers must also be sensitized to the differences in learning interests that can result from their life, career, and job changes. In a workshop, the issue of responsibility, and its positive ramifications, can be explored. In a sense, merely by addressing this issue, organizations clarify what is in it for the workers if they become more self-directed and motivated to take initiative for their own learning.

Individual Learning Style. What individuals do, feel, and think about learning incidents is commonly regarded as their learning style. Identifying individual learning styles means helping individuals understand how they learn best. Perhaps best known among various efforts to define the range of learning styles is the experiential theory of David Kolb (1984).

Kolb identifies four principal learning styles. *Accommodators* must feel and do to learn. They are intuitive, preferring trial-and-error approaches to mastering what is new to them. They like the new and challenging. They gravitate to technical or practical fields. *Convergers* must think and do to learn. They like problem solving and the practical application of ideas. They use hypothetical and deductive reasoning, although they may be poor at socializing. *Divergers* must feel and watch to learn. They are imaginative and tend to be generators of new ideas. They have broad cultural interests but are usually poor at decision making. They gravitate to the arts and humanities. *Assimilators* must think and watch to learn. They prefer designing, building, testing, and analyzing. They rely on inductive more than deductive reasoning. While poor at learning from their mistakes, they gravitate to such fields as basic science and mathematics.

The Adaptive Style Inventory, first developed by Kolb (1980), helps individuals identify their learning styles so trainers can adapt to those styles when planning OJT.

Individuals who have mastered learning how to learn meet three criteria described by Smith (1982): need, style, and training. According to Smith, "learning how to learn involves possessing, or acquiring, the knowledge and skill to learn effectively in whatever situation one encounters" (p. 19). Learners feel they need to learn, appreciate the style with which they as individuals learn (Kolb, 1984), and master effective techniques for learning through training.

Learner's New Role. The importance of self-directedness as a learner responsibility is worth emphasizing. At this point, some trainers favor introducing the steps in a new approach to OJT that goes beyond the traditional approach (McCord, 1987, p. 368) we described in Chapter One. The following list compares the two approaches.

In Traditional OJT, the Trainer	*In Learner-Directed OJT, the Learner*
• Shows learners how to perform the task	• Asks a supervisor or co-worker to demonstrate how an essential job function or task is performed
• Reviews key points	• Asks someone to explain key points about the organization, group, job, and essential job function, and takes notes
• Allows learners to watch the instructor/supervisor perform the task a second time	• Asks someone to demonstrate the performance of the essential job function so that the learner can observe it again
• Allows learners to perform the simple parts of the job	• Carries out simple job functions, noting problems encountered in the process
• Guides learners to perform the whole job	• Asks questions about problems in carrying out simple job functions and begins to perform the whole job
• Lets learners perform the whole job, but monitors their performance	• Asks for feedback from others about his or her performance on the whole job
• Releases learners from training and allows them to perform on their own	• Gains self-confidence and remains current with changing procedures, policies, or tasks

As this comparison shows, when learner-directed OJT is used, the responsibility for planning learning experiences shifts from trainer to learners, and the focus is on-the-job learning and workplace-based learning (Watkins & Marsick, 1991; Wick, 1990). However, the organization must still bear responsibility for clarifying work duties or requirements and for providing an environment that encourages real-time learning (Rothwell, 2002).

Active Listening Skills. Adults devote 45 percent of all the time they spend on communication activities to listening, but just 30 percent of their time to talking, 16 percent to reading, and 9 percent to writing (Steil, Barker, & Watson, 1983). Yet as people progress through formal schooling, they receive less formal instruction on listening than on the other communication modes. As one result, the average person is a poor listener. A classic research study conducted by Atwater (1992) revealed that, after forty-eight hours, adults remember only 25 percent of what they have heard. Moreover, hearing and listening are not synonymous, although the two are frequently confused. Hearing is passive; listening is active, requiring understanding, appreciation, and retention.

The importance of listening in OJT should be obvious. Especially when OJT is conducted through one-on-one instruction, trainees must actively listen to their trainers to learn, but they often do not listen actively. Active listening implies that the listener is wholly engaged in the listening process and pays as much attention to the spirit behind the spoken words as to their surface meanings. Common reasons for a failure to listen actively include lack of attention, confusion about meanings of words or their contexts, workplace distractions or interruptions, and interpersonal problems between trainers and learners that cause emotions to impede understanding. Many organizations offer listening skills training. However, we are not aware of research evidence that links listening skills training to increases in OJT learners' understanding and retention. Investigating the relationship between effective listening and OJT success would be a worthwhile research project, since currently that relationship must be intuited.

Begin your listening skills training by administering a quiz to learners to determine just how effectively they listen. The results of such a quiz can be surprising and can increase management interest in improving such skills. They can also build learner motivation to improve.

Accelerated Learning Techniques. Definitions of accelerated learning vary, but it is typically associated with efforts to release human potential, reawaken joy in learning, and reduce learning time. Many believe that, if only techniques for such acceleration could be harnessed, training time could be slashed, and this reasoning accounts for the growing interest in accelerated learning (Meier, 2000). Unfortunately, many professional trainers do not take the subject seriously. They associate accelerated learning techniques with superficial environmental modifications, such as changes in colors, sounds, or scents. In reality, however, accelerated learning means "more than baroque music, room arrangement, or comfortable chairs" (Clement, 1992, p. 530).

To take advantage of accelerated learning techniques, learners must discover how to tap their creativity in connection with their learning (Clement, 1990). They must also learn in psychological and physiological comfort, freed from concern that they will be ridiculed when they make the predictable mistakes that are typically made during the learning process (Hovelynk, 1998). Thus, to enhance their learning rate, learners may be given instruction on relaxation techniques and creativity enhancement methods. Clement (1992, p. 532) reports that "Schuster and Gritton (1986) have measured the effectiveness of accelerated learning and say that it produces at least 300 percent improvement in the speed and effectiveness of learning." There may thus be good reason to offer both learners and trainers instruction on accelerated learning techniques as they may apply to OJT.

Questioning Skills. The ability to ask questions is as important for learners as their ability to listen actively. Without this skill, they will have difficulty seeking clarification of what they do not understand, identifying resources to carry out their work, or securing help for problems that exceed their knowledge. The authors have even heard employers remark that they regularly assess learners on the quantity and quality of the questions they ask, using that as a gauge of motivation and intelligence. Yet rarely do people receive instruction on effective questioning techniques—although exceptions may include psychologists, teachers, professional trainers, employment interviewers, and police interrogators. Effective instruction on questioning should, at the least, focus on the differences between closed and open questions.

Closed questions begin with such words as "is," "are," "was," "were," "do," or "does." "Is that the right way?" is a simple example of a closed question. Closed questions elicit yes-and-no responses and close off further discussion. They do not stimulate thinking, but they do exert control over a discussion. Open questions begin with such words as "who," "what," "when," "where," "why," or "how." "Why do we do it that way?" is a simple example of an open question. Open questions cannot be answered by a simple yes or no; they require a more complete response. Open questions stimulate dialogue and creativity. They exert little control over a discussion, prompting others to take the lead by answering.

Summary

In this chapter we presented the essential components of training workshops designed for those who conduct or receive planned OJT. While train-the-trainer experiences are essential to the success of an OJT program, we emphasized the growing importance of helping learners assume increased responsibility for their own on-the-job learning.

In the next chapter we focus attention on discovering needs for OJT. We also introduce a useful, six-step model to guide individual trainers in planning OJT. That model may be applied to individuals even when organizational leaders do not establish an organization-wide OJT program.

PART TWO

PREPARING AND DELIVERING OJT

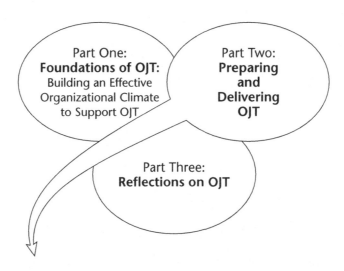

CHAPTER FIVE

DISCOVERING NEEDS

How to Determine When OJT Is Appropriate

As you establish a planned on-the-job training program, OJT trainers will ask many questions: When is OJT appropriate? How is the need for OJT discovered? On what should OJT be based? How is OJT effectively prepared, presented, and evaluated? How should other performance improvement strategies be combined or substituted for OJT? Answering these questions appropriately and accurately can spell the difference between success and failure for a planned OJT program. Even when your OJT program is not organizationwide, your on-the-job trainers will need to grapple with these questions if they are to successfully conduct OJT for individuals.

The DAPPER Model

There are six steps in the OJT process. Together they form the DAPPER model, which is the foundation for Chapters Five through Ten and which can be used to answer the questions with which we opened this chapter. The DAPPER model can also be used by individual trainers in the absence of an organization-wide OJT program. The six steps are:

1. Discover needs for planned OJT.
2. Analyze work, worker, and workplace for planned OJT.
3. Prepare planned OJT.
4. Present planned OJT.
5. Evaluate the results of planned OJT.
6. Review aids and alternatives to planned OJT.

These steps are depicted in Figure 5.1.

Once you have tentatively identified OJT as a solution for a performance problem, perform Step 1 of the DAPPER model, using performance analysis to discover your needs for OJT and to be sure OJT is appropriate for your problem (Mager & Pipe, 1997). The remainder of this chapter guides you in identifying appropriate occasions to use OJT.

Questions That Determine OJT Needs

To discover when OJT is an appropriate solution to a performance problem, test its appropriateness by answering the seventeen key questions that follow. If you answer yes to a key question, then you have probably discovered a need for OJT.

FIGURE 5.1. THE DAPPER MODEL.

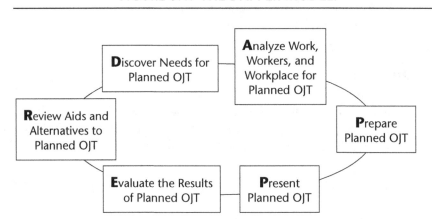

Question 1: Is the Individual New to the Organization?

To perform competently, a newly hired employee must be made aware of the employer's work rules, policies, procedures, work processes, and competitive conditions. Not all organizations face precisely the same conditions, of course, nor do all managers expect the same results from their employees. Nevertheless, all individuals entering an organization do undergo a predictable socialization period. Therefore, as soon as possible after they enter the organization, they should be informed of conditions facing the organization, management expectations, and the "way things are done here" (corporate culture) through an orientation program. Of course, they may also learn about the corporate culture from the stories they hear told in the organization (Evans & Metzger, 2000). The orientation should also provide some basis for the OJT that will follow it. The key issues that should be reviewed in any organizational orientation are the following:

- Type of organization
- Organizational affiliation/relationship to other organizations
- Organizational size and place in the industry
- Customers served and their needs
- Organizational mission/purpose
- Competitive challenges faced by the organization
- Strategic plans of the organization
- Organizational products and/or services
- Organizational chart/reporting relationships
- Organizational facilities and locations
- Equipment used by the organization
- Human resource policies and procedures
    - Full-time versus part-time employment
    - Recruitment
    - Selection
    - Orientation
    - Compensation
    - Employee benefit policies (life, health, disability, pension)
    - Equal employment opportunity and affirmative action
    - Training
    - Promotion/transfer
    - Performance appraisal

- Discipline and discharge
- Safety program and hazardous substances
- Medical issue

Much attention has been focused around orientation in recent years (see Sharpe, 1997). Some observers properly position it as an assimilation or socialization process (George & Miller, 1996)—not a one-shot event or course—that gradually helps newcomers (or those promoted) adapt to a new setting. That is particularly important in firms such as KPMG Peat Marwick, where the cost to hire averages $30,000 to $50,000 and so keeping turnover low is important for cost control (Winkler & Janger, 1998). Some observers argue that orientation should be viewed as part of a process that begins with recruitment and selection and extends through organizational orientation, individual OJT, and follow-on training (Brull, 1999; Lachnit, 2002). Orientation programs may be conducted live, although increasing interest focuses around online methods of providing information (Dobbs, 2001; Westwood & Johnson, 2002), brick-and-mortar or virtual learning centers in which individuals can stop by for help at the time they need it (Piskurich, 1999), online learning communities in which individuals can get help from more experienced people or supervisors in real time (Boxer & Johnson, 2002; Newman & Smith, 1999; Russell, 1999), and communities of practice in which people can share what they learn (Stamps, 1997a, 1997b). Some favor a military-style boot camp experience for newcomers (Brandel, 1999; Brinkley & Florian, 1998; Tichy, 2001).

Many case studies have been written to describe organizational orientation programs, and they are worth reviewing to glean best practices from them. See, for instance, the description of orientation for Hewlett-Packard, Corning, and Microstrategy in Garvey (2001). Dobbs (2001) describes the online orientation programs at IBM, KPMG, and click2learn.com. Birchard (1997) reviews orientation at Netscape, Cisco, and Yahoo. Hemp (2002) describes first-hand experience with orientation at the Ritz-Carlton hotel. Weber (1999) reviews a comprehensive program at PriceWaterhouseCooper that includes new employee orientation. Ganzel (1998) describes orientation programs at Southwest Airlines, Quad/Graphics, Ernst and Young, IBM, and System One. Rubis (1998) discusses how Walt Disney World orients new hires.

An organizational orientation should not be necessary for veteran employees, assuming they have been kept informed of changing conditions in the organization. The numerous books and articles about orientation programs are a source of useful ideas for establishing a program where one does not exist.

Question 2: Is the Individual New to the Division or Department?

Just as newly hired employees deserve an organizational orientation, employees who move from one division or department to another within an organization deserve an orientation to their new area because work rules, policies, procedures, and work processes are not always applied in precisely the same way across an organization and even across shifts in the same organization. Differing work demands, management styles and values, and traditions usually account for these variations.

Key employee questions that should be answered in a divisional or departmental orientation are these:

- What is the division's or department's purpose or mission?
- How long has the division or department existed?
- Why was the division or department created?
- What is the division or department's unique contribution to the organization?
- Why is that contribution important?
- Who are the customers served by the division or department?
- What do the customers need, expect, or require?
- How is the division or department structured?
- What does each work unit do?
- Who are the leaders of the division or department?
- What do the leaders do?
- What unique policies, procedures, or work requirements exist in the division or department?

Question 3: Is the Individual New to the Work Unit?

It is difficult for a newcomer to a work unit to appreciate how he or she can contribute to it without first knowing its purpose, scope of duties, customers, rules, policies, and procedures. This knowledge is especially important for employees joining work teams in which team members must function cohesively, interchangeably, and interdependently. For this reason, newcomers to each work unit should be oriented to it, just as newcomers are oriented to an organization, division, or department.

There are at least two approaches to organizing a work unit orientation. The first is to use a planned training method, carried out by a supervisor, team leader, or an experienced co-worker. Armed with a checklist or lesson plan, the trainer instructs the newcomer on key work unit issues early on, perhaps during the first

EXHIBIT 5.1. WORK UNIT ORIENTATION CHECKLIST.

Job Title: Date:
Employee: Department:

Directions for the supervisor: Complete this checklist for each newcomer to a work unit as soon as possible after he or she begins work. On completion, ask the new employee to sign the checklist. Give the employee a copy and return the original to your human resources person or department for inclusion in the employee's personnel file.

Did you discuss the following issues with the new employee?	Yes	No	N/A	Notes
1. Work unit's purpose/relationship to the organization?	( )	( )	( )	
2. Work unit's structure/jobs?	( )	( )	( )	
3. Work unit's customers and their needs?	( )	( )	( )	
4. Work unit's challenges/pressures?	( )	( )	( )	
5. The newcomer's job?	( )	( )	( )	
6. Job performance standards?	( )	( )	( )	
7. On-the-job training?	( )	( )	( )	
8. Unit policies on				
Safety and health?	( )	( )	( )	
Dress code?	( )	( )	( )	
Attendance?	( )	( )	( )	
Breaks?	( )	( )	( )	
Hours of work?	( )	( )	( )	
Discipline?	( )	( )	( )	
Overtime?	( )	( )	( )	
Parking?	( )	( )	( )	
Appraisal and salary?	( )	( )	( )	
Telephone use?	( )	( )	( )	
Visitors?	( )	( )	( )	
Vacation time/scheduling?	( )	( )	( )	
9. Key people to meet?	( )	( )	( )	
10. Key places to see?	( )	( )	( )	
11. Other matters (list here)				

Employee   Date

Supervisor   Date

Mastering the Instructional Design Process: A Systematic Approach, Third Edition. Copyright © 2004 by John Wiley & Sons, Inc. Reproduced by permission of Pfeiffer, an Imprint of Wiley. www.pfeiffer.com

day or first week. Exhibit 5.1 contains a checklist that a supervisor or team leader can use to orient a newcomer to a work unit.

The second approach is to organize a means by which newcomers can conduct their own work unit orientations. As a starting point, the trainer can ask the newcomer to take the initiative to find the answers to such questions as those posed on the checklist in Exhibit 5.1. The trainer can then ask the newcomer to plot the work flow into, through, and out of the work unit, as a form of organizational mapping.

As a simple example of this orientation assignment, suppose that an insurance company employee joins a small specialized work unit of six people. Each worker in the unit performs different activities, and the work flows from desk to desk–much as a product on an assembly line flows from station to station. The newcomer could be given a chart of the desks and asked to fill in "who does what" (see Exhibit 5.2).

EXHIBIT 5.2. CHARTING WORK UNIT WORK FLOW.

Job Title: Date:
Employee:

1. Describe the work as it enters the unit:

2. In the spaces below, describe work performed at each desk:

3. Describe the work as it leaves the unit. Who uses the outputs? What are their expectations or needs?

Employee   Date

Supervisor   Date

Additionally, a newcomer to a work unit may be directed to explore such issues as these:

- Who are the customers of the work unit? How do they view its activities?
- Where does the work of the unit come from? In what state is the work received?
- How do work processes branch into different activities depending on what must be done?
- Who does what in the unit, and why?
- What improvements might be made to the unit's work inputs, processes, and outputs in your opinion? What led you to think of these improvements?

During work unit orientation, a newcomer may also be assigned a peer mentor (who will be different from the assigned job trainer), who will help the newcomer fit into the work unit's social structure. The peer mentor's role is to introduce the newcomer to co-workers *and* to make him or her feel welcome. By using a peer mentor system, units may be able to hold down turnover statistics as well as encourage the informal networking that is so important to workplace learning (Charney, 1996; Nilson, 1990).

Question 4: Is the Individual New to the Job?

Most newcomers to a job will require some OJT, even when they have performed similar work in other contexts. When an individual is new to the job, the trainer should take time to learn about him or her. What is known about the person from the recruitment and selection process? Why was this person selected? What education, training, or experience does the individual bring to the job; that is, what does the individual already know? What does he or she need to learn about the occupation, job, or organizational or work unit culture? The trainer must take the answers to these questions into account as OJT is planned for the individual.

Question 5: Does the Individual Lack Knowledge of the Essential Job Functions?

Before OJT can be carried out, job functions must be clarified at the organizational level. Job incumbents should know what they will be expected to do before they are trained to do it or held fully accountable for it. Unfortunately, not all organizations clarify the essential functions of each job, although the requirements of the Americans with Disabilities Act have made it more common for them to do so. When organizational leaders or work unit supervisors do not know or agree on what the essential job functions should be, then work analysis is clearly warranted to clarify the functions and provide a basis for briefing job incumbents. Of course, work analysis is also conducted for other reasons, such as establishing a basis for recruitment, selection, wages, and other employment decisions. (For information about conducting work analysis, see Chapter Six.) Only by clarifying work requirements and essential job functions will workers know what what they are expected to do.

Question 6: Does the Individual Lack Ability to Perform Essential Job Functions?

Reading a job description is not the same as performing job functions. If individuals already know how to perform the job properly and have done so in the past, then they do not need training. If they do not know how to perform it, then the trainer should establish an OJT plan and schedule based on the job description and, if possible, on the more detailed information that can be obtained through more time-consuming methods such as task analysis. (Task analysis is detailed in Chapter Seven.)

Question 7: Does the Individual Lack Knowledge of When to Perform?

You would not dream of answering a telephone unless it rang first (and if you behaved otherwise, people would wonder about your sanity). Answering a business telephone is a work routine that begins only when the ringing of the telephone alerts the performer to an appropriate occasion to perform. Almost all work routines are started because the worker receives some sort of signal. Individuals must know these signals, know *when* it is appropriate for them to carry out essential job functions. In some cases, as the telephone example illustrates, a machine signal alerts the performer to the occasion to perform. In other cases—particularly in tasks associated with professional, technical, or managerial work—performers may exercise considerable discretion in deciding when to perform a work activity. Perhaps they wait until customer complaints eventually signal the need to act. Perhaps they receive no external cue to perform at all. Even in these latter cases, however, workers must still have a sense of when it is and is not appropriate to carry out each job function. If workers have previously demonstrated familiarity with appropriate occasions to perform, then they may not need OJT and may benefit from practice or reminders instead. If the trainer is not sure when performance is warranted, exemplary workers may shed light on the cues they themselves use to determine appropriate occasions to perform. (If even exemplary workers cannot explain how they determine when to perform, then redesigning the job to create performance cues may be justified.)

Question 8: Does the Individual Lack Knowledge of Measurable Job Performance Standards?

Not long ago, some U.S. companies were accused of shoddy workmanship in their products and services. Today, they have recognized that consumers are as interested in quality as they are in the product or service itself. Thus, U.S. companies are devoting increasing attention to organizational and individual performance standards or measures of acceptability, evaluating worker performance by such measures as quantity and quality of output and cost, time, and complaint rates. However, workers cannot meet an organization's measurable job performance standards if standards have not been established or if the workers do not know the standards. As you investigate your organization's need for OJT, then, one issue to consider is individuals' awareness of how results are measured. Do individuals understand the measurable job performance standards linked to each job function? If standards are lacking, they should be established. If standards are in place, they should be clearly communicated as the job performance standards against which workers may be held accountable. This communication may be given during OJT or separately.

Question 9: Does the Individual Lack Knowledge of Why the Job Functions Are Important?

Individuals are not always aware of the consequences that will stem from what they do or how important those consequences may be. For instance, performers may not be aware of how their work contributes to what co-workers do or how it affects the organization's customers. As a result, they may not appreciate the importance of their work or take pride in their workmanship. Therefore, it is important that they understand why they do what they do and why their work is important. They deserve an explanation of the role played by their job functions, and this explanation can be planned to be part of OJT.

Question 10: Does the Individual Lack Knowledge of Where Job Functions Should Be Performed?

Just as individuals should be aware of *when* to perform, they should also be aware of *where* to perform. Some work tasks should not be carried out if necessary tools, equipment, or other support materials are lacking. To take an extreme example, a physician would not perform surgery in a pasture, because sterile conditions would be compromised and the surgical instruments and other supports necessary for a successful operation, such as anesthesia and respiratory equipment, would presumably be lacking.

When performers do not know where (in what setting or with what tools and equipment) it is appropriate for them to carry out a job function, they should be instructed, and that instruction can be performed as part of OJT.

Question 11: Does the Individual Have a Different Learning Need from the Group?

If an individual has needs that are different from the group's needs then OJT is probably called for. If the group shares the individual's learning needs, then group instruction in a classroom or online may be more appropriate and cost effective than OJT conducted one-on-one. If instruction is presented off-the-job, however, close attention should be paid to ensure that individuals are held accountable for what they learn and that adequate transfer of learning occurs from classroom to workplace (Baldwin & Ford, 1988).

Most trainers find that some issues are better presented in the classroom, while others are better presented on the job. For instance, as a result of regulations issued by the Occupational Safety and Health Administration, all workers in the United States should receive some safety training on hazardous substances. Such training may be cost-effectively presented through off-the-shelf or computer-based training packages that are available from commercial publishers and lend themselves to modification for in-house use. Once on-the-job trainers have determined that some issues may be successfully treated in the classroom rather than on the job, these issues can be separated out from OJT needs for preparation and presentation. Any one of numerous books on the subject of instructional design can guide your preparation and presentation (Rothwell and Kazonas, 2004).

Question 12: Have Job Functions Changed, or Are They About to Change?

Change is the only constant in today's dynamic workplaces. Job functions do not remain the same forever. As a result, workers' knowledge and skills must be updated quickly and continuously. OJT is uniquely suited to fast deployment and can provide tailored, individualized instruction that is difficult to match through alternative methods.

When job functions change, workers must be made aware of what those changes will be and how they will affect performance. For example, if new work processes or equipment are to be installed, what impact will they have on how and when the work should be carried out? If new laws, rules, or regulations will affect the organization's policies and procedures, what effects will those changes exert on job performance? Once those questions can be answered, prepare and present OJT so that workers can be kept abreast of new job performance expectations.

Question 13: Have Performance Obstacles in the Work Environment Been Removed?

Do obstacles prevent individuals from performing competently? Do they lack the right tools, equipment, or other resources to perform? Are they unintentionally punished for performing, rewarded for not performing, or given no incentive to perform as desired? If obstacles exist that inhibit effective performance, then you must remove them (Mager & Pipe, 1997). However, if they have been removed and the performance problem persists, then OJT may be appropriate.

Question 14: Is OJT More Cost-Effective Than Other Solutions?

Training, whether delivered in the classroom or on the job, should properly be regarded as the employee performance improvement strategy of last resort (Rothwell & Kazanas, 2004). Training is an expensive intervention, and other methods may often be cost-effectively substituted for it. Employee performance improvement strategies that may be substituted for, or used in conjunction with, OJT include changing employee selection methods, improving the timeliness and clarity of performance feedback given to employees, improving the match between incentive/reward systems and performance goals, restructuring the organization to improve work flow, and redesigning jobs by moving responsibilities or tasks from one job to another. As you can see, these noninstructional interventions generally focus less on what employees need to know to perform (the focus of OJT and other instructional interventions) and more on what management should do to organize the work, select workers, furnish clear and timely information, and provide performance incentives.

Various aids to performance may also be paired up with, or substituted for OJT presented through one-on-one instruction. Examples of such aids are procedure manuals, training manuals and outlines, computer-based training, employee and supervisory checklists, and electronic performance support systems (EPSS). Many of these aids will be discussed in Chapter Nine. For now, simply be aware that they can either substitute for, or complement, OJT. If they cannot be substituted, then OJT is probably appropriate.

Question 15: Can Workplace Distractions Be Minimized?

Because people must concentrate to learn, OJT should be used only when distractions in the workplace can be minimized. If people are continually interrupted and thus unable to concentrate, they will not be able to take full advantage of organized instruction.

Question 16: Can Workplace Health and Safety Hazards Be Minimized?

If workers' health and safety will not be compromised while an individual learns on the job, then OJT may be appropriate. However, if health and safety hazards cannot be minimized, alternative performance improvement strategies should be used.

Question 17: Can Adequate Time, Staff, and Other Resources Be Devoted to OJT?

If OJT has not been ruled out by an earlier question, and you have the time, staff, and other necessary resources to commit to OJT, then you are ready to use it for the needs you have defined. Move on to the next step of the DAPPER model, and prepare to analyze work, worker, and workplace.

Summary

OJT trainers will ask many questions as they establish a planned on-the-job training program. This chapter posed seventeen of those questions and offered answers to them. The questions were:

- Question 1: Is the Individual New to the Organization?
- Question 2: Is the Individual New to the Division or Department?
- Question 3: Is the Individual New to the Work Unit?
- Question 4: Is the Individual New to the Job?
- Question 5: Does the Individual Lack Knowledge of the Essential Job Functions?
- Question 6: Does the Individual Lack Ability to Perform Essential Job Functions?
- Question 7: Does the Individual Lack Knowledge of When to Perform?
- Question 8: Does the Individual Lack Knowledge of Measurable Job Performance Standards?
- Question 9: Does the Individual Lack Knowledge of Why the Job Functions Are Important?
- Question 10: Does the Individual Lack Knowledge of Where Job Functions Should Be Performed?
- Question 11: Does the Individual Have a Different Learning Need from the Group?

- Question 12: Have Job Functions Changed, or Are They About to Change?
- Question 13: Have Performance Obstacles in the Work Environment Been Removed?
- Question 14: Is OJT More Cost-Effective Than Other Solutions?
- Question 15: Can Workplace Distractions Be Minimized?
- Question 16: Can Workplace Health and Safety Hazards Be Minimized?
- Question 17: Can Adequate Time, Staff, and Other Resources Be Devoted to OJT?

The next chapter focuses on the second step in the DAPPER model: analyzing the work, worker, and workplace. It briefly explains ways to go about the analysis of what work people do, the kind of people who do the work, and the nature of the work environment in which learners will apply what they learn. Taking those into account is essential for a good OJT program.

CHAPTER SIX

ANALYZING WORK, WORKER, AND WORKPLACE

How to Fit the Training to the Job

Once you have discovered a need for on-the-job training, turn to the second step in the DAPPER model: analyzing the work, worker, and workplace. Planned OJT should be solidly based on what workers are expected to do, their individual capabilities, and the conditions of the work environment in which they will perform. Work, worker, and workplace analysis will supply you with the information you require to make OJT effective.

Work Analysis

Take the following six steps to develop an up-to-date work analysis, or job description. These steps may be performed by a supervisor, job incumbent, team member, human resource specialist, in-house training professional, vendor, or another person.

Step 1: Collect Background Information

Collection of background information about the job to be analyzed begins with an organization chart and copies of previously prepared descriptions of the job. If possible, also locate comparable job descriptions in the *Dictionary of Occupational Titles* (1977)—which can be found on the web under "job genie" (see www.stepfour.com/jobs/)—or its more recent web-based counterpart called the

Occupational Information Resource Network (otherwise known as O'Net; see www.onetcenter.org/). If you wish, you may also locate job descriptions through benchmarking efforts, using copies of comparable job descriptions prepared in other organizations. Use your organization chart to clarify reporting relationships and the job's placement in the chain of command. Use the previously prepared job descriptions to compile an initial list of essential job functions (this will slash the time required to identify obvious functions). Use the comparable job descriptions to clarify how those outside the organization have described the job. For more detailed information about work analysis, see Brannick and Levine (2002) and Hartley (1999).

Step 2: Develop a Work Plan

The work plan you develop will guide your work analysis. The plan should include the objectives to be achieved in the work analysis and the job description format to be used. Exhibit 6.1 contains a format for a job description, and Exhibit 6.2 is a sample job description in that format. Some organizations prefer to establish and consistently use their own formats, though various formats are available (see Plachy & Plachy, 1993).

 EXHIBIT 6.1. FORMAT FOR A JOB DESCRIPTION.

	(Organization Name)	
Job Title:	Classification:	Pay Grade:
Department:	Budget Center:	
Summary:		

Approximate hours spent per week

1. List essential job functions:
2. List nonessential job functions:
3. List skills required:
4. List working conditions:

Written by	Date

Approved by	Date

Employee currently performing job	Date

EXHIBIT 6.2. SAMPLE JOB DESCRIPTION.

Organization's Name

Job Title: Receptionist   **Pay Grade:** 2   **Job Code:** E742
Department: Human Resources   **Budget Center:** 1423

Summary: It is the responsibility of the receptionist in the Human Resources Department to interact with applicants and company employees in a friendly and courteous manner and to achieve all essential functions as outlined in the job description.

1. List essential job functions:

Approximate Hours Spent Per Week

☐ Makes applicants feel welcome and ensures that applicants
   successfully complete applications   5
☐ Furnishes information to appropriate people regarding
   employment matters   6.5
☐ Keeps personnel files up-to-date   10
☐ Provides payments to employees and vendors based on company
   accounting requirements   2
☐ Provides information to past and present employees in accordance
   with company procedures   2
☐ Provides Employment Manager with typed letters for signature   5
☐ Answers multi-line phone and directs calls to appropriate personnel
   throughout the Human Resources Department and company   3

2. List nonessential job functions:
☐ Ensures appropriate employment tests are administered and results are received
☐ Ensures that paperwork for new employees is properly completed
☐ Maintains personnel records for all employees in the company
☐ Supplies all employees with nameplates
☐ Ensures that conference rooms are scheduled correctly
☐ Provides to our compensation representatives copies of report when individuals file
   for unemployment compensation
☐ Ensures that all terminating employees are scheduled for exit interviews
☐ Ensures that Human Resources personnel have the proper office supplies with which
   to complete their work assignments
☐ Keeps accurate information regarding job applicants
☐ Reimburses company employees for money lost in vending machines
☐ Alerts officers and managers of current job opportunities in conformance
   with the company's job posting policy
☐ Alerts company personnel of funeral arrangements for employees' family members
☐ Ensures that all applicants are aware that their applications and/or resumes have been
   received
☐ Maintains attendance in line with company requirements, arrives at work
   on a timely and consistent basis, uses language properly and courteously,
   maintains job performance consistent with established measurable job
   performance standards and company requirements, exhibits honesty, and maintains
   harmonious working relationships with others

Note: This list is not exhaustive and may be supplemented as necessary.

continued

EXHIBIT 6.2. SAMPLE JOB DESCRIPTION (continued).

3. List skills required:
   - ☐ Speaks and writes clearly
   - ☐ Stands and bends approximately 10 hours weekly
   - ☐ Presents a pleasant personality and good interpersonal skills appropriate for greeting applicants and company personnel
   - ☐ Handles multiple work priorities effectively
   - ☐ Demonstrates ability to work with details and organize assigned paperwork
   - ☐ Types 35 to 40 words per minute with 3 errors or fewer

4. List working conditions:
   No unusual working conditions; works in an office environment

Written by   Date

Approved by   Date

Employee currently performing job   Date

When developing your work plan, be sure to consider the following questions:

- How should work analysis be carried out?
- How much time, money, and effort are available to conduct the study?
- What special preferences, if any, do management or labor representatives have about the way work analysis is to be conducted?
- What information is desired from the work analysis? More specifically, which of the following types of information are to be obtained:
   Job title
   Location of the job
   Essential job functions
   Tools or equipment needed
   Estimated time spent on each job function, duty, task, or activity by job incumbents
   Importance (criticality) of each function to job success, health, safety, or customer satisfaction
   Standards, measurable or otherwise, describing how well each job function is to be performed
   Physical, mental, emotional, or learning demands of each essential job function
   Knowledge, skills, or abilities necessary to carry out job functions

- What sample of job incumbents should be used?
- How will the information gathered be analyzed and verified?
- How will conflicts about the results be resolved, and by whom?

Step 3: Conduct Briefings

The appropriate organizational stakeholders must be briefed about the work analysis and approaches to be used. First, identify the stakeholders most interested in the results. (Examples of stakeholders might include the supervisor, the worker, union representatives, HR representatives, and others.) Clarify what they want to learn from the analysis–and why they want to learn it–and check to be sure the work plan will yield the desired results. Finally, determine how to explain the benefits of work analysis to key stakeholders.

Step 4: Select an Information-Gathering Approach

Select an information-gathering approach likely to yield the desired information within existing time, money, and staffing constraints. As part of this step, consider past work analysis studies conducted in your organization and identify especially effective or ineffective approaches. In addition, consider these two questions: What methods can be used to ensure maximum participation and cooperation from the participants? How can stakeholder participation and cooperation be maintained?

Work analysis information may be gathered through various approaches. Observation, individual interviews, group interviews, written questionnaires, diaries, computerized conferences, audio teleconferences, videoconferences, critical incident reporting, and the DACUM method are useful approaches that are summarized in the following paragraphs.

Observation requires the person gathering information to watch people as they carry out their jobs. An effective observer should:

1. Review previous job descriptions and studies.
2. Choose representative job incumbents to observe, briefing them and their immediate supervisors about the study and reasons for undertaking it.
3. Prepare a behavior observation form to capture information about work functions, duties, tasks, or activities performed.
4. Visit the work site on a predetermined schedule to observe work as it is performed.

The advantage of observation by a third party is that it captures what really happens, not what job incumbents or their immediate supervisors only perceive or want to be happening. The disadvantages are that it is expensive and time-consuming to conduct and that not all job activities are easily observed.

Individual interviews focus on questioning job incumbents one at a time about a job's functions. To be successful, information gatherers should:

1. Review previous job descriptions and similar studies.
2. Choose representative job incumbents to interview, briefing them and their immediate supervisors about the study and reasons for undertaking it.
3. Prepare a structured interview guide to capture information about job functions, duties, tasks, or activities.
4. Visit the work site to interview job incumbent(s) and/or supervisor(s).
5. Feed interview results back to respondents to verify results.

The advantages to individual interviews are that the findings are not swayed by a few especially vocal individuals, as may happen in group interviews, and that experienced job incumbents are knowledgeable about the job functions. The disadvantages are that individual interviews are expensive to conduct, requiring travel to individual work sites by a trained interviewer, and that they tend to capture information about a job as it is perceived rather than objectively observed.

Group interviews pose questions about work performed to a group of job incumbents and/or their supervisors. A successful group interviewer should:

1. Review previous job descriptions and studies performed.
2. Choose representative job incumbents or supervisors to participate and brief them about the reasons for the job study.
3. Prepare an agenda to guide the meeting.
4. Start the meeting by explaining the purpose of the job analysis, how results will and will not be used, and how the group interview will proceed.
5. Ask workers and/or supervisors to describe what they do.
6. List the activities described.
7. Verify the activities by asking participants to review/modify the functions, duties, tasks, or activities they identified.

The advantage to group interviews is that, through group synergy, groups identify more job activities and do it faster than individuals can. Disadvantages are that group interviews may be dominated by one or two individuals, thereby skewing the results, and that such interviews are costly because they take a number of productive workers or supervisors away from production activities.

You can use a commercially available written *questionnaire* or develop your own to collect information about job functions, duties, tasks, or activities. To apply this approach successfully, an information gatherer should:

1. Review previous job descriptions and studies.
2. Choose representative job incumbents and/or supervisors to participate in the job analysis study and brief them about the data collection method.
3. Draft a written questionnaire or pilot test a commercially available instrument such as the Position Analysis Questionnaire (PAQ).
4. Test the questionnaire to ensure questions are clear and elicit the desired information.
5. Ask workers and/or supervisors to complete the written questionnaire, describing what they do.
6. List the activities described.
7. Verify the activities by asking participants to review/modify the functions, duties, tasks, or activities they identified.

Written questionnaires are inexpensive to use and also have the advantage of obtaining information from many people in a short time. Their disadvantages are that their success depends on the clarity of the written questions and the writing skills of the respondents.

Diaries require one or more job incumbents to periodically track their work activities. To get usable results from diaries, the information gatherer should:

1. Review previous job descriptions and studies.
2. Choose representative job incumbents and/or supervisors to participate in the job analysis study and brief them about the need for the study.
3. Draft a diary/log that solicits information about duties, functions, tasks, or activities on some periodic basis, such as every fifteen or thirty minutes or every hour.
4. Test the diary/log to ensure that it is understandable to users and elicits desired information.
5. Ask workers and/or supervisors to use the diary/log to describe what they do.
6. List work activities described.
7. Verify activities by asking participants to review/modify the functions, duties, tasks, and activities they identified.

Computerized conferences use such computer technology as electronic mail, message boards, and web-based software to collect work analysis information. A simple search on the web should uncover many examples of such products. They may be synchronous (in which everyone meets together online at once) or asynchronous (in which everyone periodically provides information to a static site such as an electronic bulletin board). To create and use an electronic mail questionnaire, follow the actions described for creating and using a written questionnaire. In addition to the advantages and disadvantages mentioned for the written questionnaire, a computerized conference has the disadvantages of being unsuitable for people who have no access to electronic mail or who feel threatened by computers.

Audio teleconferences use telephone technology to ask many people at one time for work analysis information. A teleconference is designed and implemented like a group interview and also shares the advantages and disadvantages of a group interview. To conduct such an interview, it is usually necessary to arrange a time when people can meet on the phone. It may be necessary to send the questions in advance by e-mail or fax. Since people have a low tolerance for teleconferences, it is usually wise to try to keep them as short as possible.

In the years since the first edition of this book was published, *videoconferences* have become much more popular. They can be run just like an audioconference but require additional software (such as Microsoft NetMeeting®). Like audio teleconferences, they work best if kept short and focused.

Critical incident reports allow experienced job incumbents to describe situations (incidents) that are especially important (critical) to effective job performance. To get appropriate reports, the information gatherer should:

1. Select a panel of experienced job incumbents and/or their immediate supervisors.
2. Assemble the panel in a meeting or draft a written survey to collect information about critical incidents.
3. Brief panel members on:
   - The critical incident method
   - The way they were selected for participation
   - The purpose of the job analysis
   - The way(s) the results will be used
4. Ask panel members to:
   - Describe a situation they encountered in the past that was especially easy or difficult
   - Describe how they handled the situation
   - Describe how they would handle the situation if they encountered it again
5. Compare critical incidents supplied by the panel as a means of identifying especially important work activities.
6. Feed results of the study back to participants as a basis for verifying especially important work activities.

The advantages of the critical incident approach are its great appeal to experienced workers and supervisors and its focus on the most important aspects of job activities. Its disadvantages are that it covers work activities unevenly, favoring the difficult or unusual over the routine, and it tends not to yield results suitable for use in a job description.

DACUM is an acronym for "developing a curriculum," and the DACUM method uses a committee of experienced job incumbents to identify work functions, duties, tasks, and activities and to sequence them by difficulty as a prelude to task analysis (Jonassen, Hannum, & Tessmer, 1989).

The investigator should follow either the actions described for the group interviews or these actions described by Norton (1997):

1. Orient the DACUM committee to what the method is.
2. Examine what information is known about the job.
3. Prompt members of the committee to list the work activities.
4. Clarify what tasks are performed for each work activity.
5. Provide a summary of the work activities and tasks.
6. Sequence activities and tasks by how difficult they are to learn or perform.

The DACUM method has most of the same advantages and disadvantages as the group interview. However, a key advantage is that the work activities to which a newcomer is introduced can be sequenced according to the expert opinion of experienced job incumbents. The method can also be a tool for developing measurable job performance standards. (See Fetterman [1996] for a description of how DACUM has been used to certify in-house instructors at Pennsylvania Power and Light.)

Note that it is possible to combine the methods. That often works best because it leads to an ability to doublecheck the results of the methods that are combined. (Researchers give that the name *triangulation*.) It may even supply additional, useful information. For instance, the DACUM method does a good job of identifying what people do on a daily basis, while the critical incident approach is particularly effective in identifying highly unusual–and perhaps critically important–situations that may lead to exemplary or egregious performance.

Step 5: Draft a Job Description

Use the results of the work analysis to draft the job description. Then identify exemplary or experienced job incumbents and give them the draft job description for comment. Modify the draft job description based on feedback and suggested modifications from these incumbents and such other key stakeholders as the supervisor or a human resources department representative.

Step 6: Prepare Final Job Description

Put the results of your information gathering in final form by preparing an up-to-date job description, and present this job description to job incumbents, management and labor representatives, and other interested parties. Take steps to ensure that the job description is periodically reviewed and updated as working conditions change.

Of course, steps may be added or deleted from this work analysis process to tailor it to specific organizational and user needs. For example, a supervisor who is preparing OJT for one newcomer may decide to simplify the process by first updating the job description and then using the questions shown on the work analysis worksheet in Exhibit 6.3. (Use Exhibit 6.4 to answer the last question on the worksheet.) We cannot overemphasize the importance of answering these questions. The answers that result from this practical and easily performed exercise are the foundation for developing an effective plan and schedule to guide most OJT.

 EXHIBIT 6.3. WORK ANALYSIS WORKSHEET.

Job Title: Date:
Department:

Directions: Once you have selected the job for which you want to prepare OJT, use the current job description to answer the following questions. (The process begun on this worksheet will probably require many pages to complete.)

1. *What* should the worker do? (List the essential and nonessential job functions.)
2. *How* should the worker perform work tasks or activities? (List tasks or key steps for performing each essential and nonessential job function.)
3. *When* should workers perform? (List performance cues.)
4. *Why* should workers perform? (List the consequences/importance of each essential job function.)
5. *Where* should workers perform? (Name the appropriate locale for performing each job function.)
6. *How well* should workers perform? (List the measurable job performance standards or expectations linked to each job function.)

Written by   Date

Approved by   Date

Employee currently performing job   Date

EXHIBIT 6.4. THREE CATEGORIES IN WHICH TO ESTABLISH MEASURABLE JOB PERFORMANCE STANDARDS.

1. **Quality.** Measure these elements:

   ☐ *Accuracy*: Degree to which an accomplishment matches a model.

   ☐ *Class*: Comparative superiority of one accomplishment over another based on market value, judgment points, physical measures, and opinion ratings.

   ☐ *Novelty*: Uniqueness of the accomplishment.

   ☐ *Combinations*: Linking together of more than one quality class.

2. **Quantity/Productivity.** Measure these elements:

   ☐ *Rate.* The number of items or pieces produced within a specific time period.

   ☐ *Timeliness.* The completion of an accomplishment within a specified time limit.

   ☐ *Volume.* The amount of the accomplishment, but is not rate or time dependent.

3. **Cost**

   ☐ *Labor.* The amount expended on labor to make an accomplishment.

   ☐ *Material.* The material costs required to make an accomplishment.

   ☐ *Management.* The managerial and administrative costs associated with an accomplishment.

Source: Jacobs, R. *Human Performance Technology: A Systems-Based Field for the Training and Development Profession.* Columbus, OH: The National Center for Research in Vocational Education, 1987, p. 15. Adapted from Gilbert, T. *Human Competence: Engineering Worthy Performance.* New York: McGraw-Hill, 1978.

Worker Analysis

While work analysis provides critically important information that serves as the basis for training workers in essential functions, there is little point to preparing and presenting an identical form of OJT to all workers sharing the same job title. Individuals differ in education, experience, knowledge, skill, attitude, motivation, interest, talent, learning styles–and generation (Knight, 1999). A chief strength of planned OJT is that you can gear it to individual learning needs in a way that is often impossible in group settings. For example, an OJT trainer may choose to omit background information that is unnecessary for one newcomer in order to focus instead on the specific functions or problems that particular newcomer faces. To obtain the pertinent job-related information about an individual that will allow a supervisor, experienced co-worker, or other trainer to gear training to that individual's learning needs, a worker analysis must be performed.

The secret to effective worker analysis lies in discovering precisely how well the individual who is to receive OJT is already able to perform essential job functions and the activities associated with each function, recognize performance cues associated with each job function, appreciate why performance is necessary (that is, understand work consequences), recognize and take into account necessary requirements for performance, and meet measurable job performance standards.

You establish worker analysis parameters by taking the following nine steps. Use the results of work analysis to guide the recruitment and selection process. Since what a worker brings to a job affects the length and depth of OJT required, the training period can be reduced by hiring, if possible, an applicant already possessing the necessary knowledge, skills, or attitudes to carry out the essential job functions.

Step 1: Prepare an Ideal Job Candidate Profile

Use the essential job functions on the job description as a starting point to prepare an ideal job candidate profile. For each essential job function, list the knowledge, skills, and attitudes that are required. Organize the candidate profile by listing job functions in one column and the corresponding knowledge, skills, or attitudes in a second column (see Exhibit 6.5). To identify needed skills, shop through published lists of job skills (like the ones shown in Exhibit 6.6) and then add other skills as necessary.

EXHIBIT 6.5. IDEAL JOB CANDIDATE PROFILE.

Job Title: Date:

Directions: To clarify the knowledge and skills required for a worker to perform job functions, list the job functions in the left-hand column, using the current job description. List the worker knowledge or skill required to perform the function in the right-hand column. (The process begun on this worksheet will probably require many pages to complete.) When you are finished, show the results to one or more experienced job incumbents and ask for their comments.

What are the job functions?   What knowledge or skills are required for workers to perform those functions?

Supervisor   Date

Trainer   Date

Experienced job incumbent   Date

Mastering the Instructional Design Process: A Systematic Approach, Third Edition. Copyright © 2004 by John Wiley & Sons, Inc. Reproduced by permission of Pfeiffer, an Imprint of Wiley. www.pfeiffer.com

EXHIBIT 6.6. SKILL-BASED JOB
ANALYSIS TAXONOMY.

Language Skills
- Reading comprehension
- Applied reading skills
- Referencing written materials
- Forms completion
- Preparation of written reading materials

Math Skills
- Table amd graph comprehension
- Arithmetic computation
- Arithmetic reasoning
- Algebra
- Advanced math skills
- Measurement
- Applied statistics

Analytical Skills
- Planning and organizing
- Active listening
- Classifying
- Analyzing
- Estimating
- Judgment
- Troubleshooting
- Innovation

Perceptual Skills
- Checking
- Inspection
- Monitoring
- Controlling
- Spatial visualization

Learning and Memory Skills
- Procedures learning
- Applied learning
- Memory

Technological Literacy
- Instrumentation
- Machine and equipment operation
- Diagram and blueprint
- Table and graph preparation
- Pictorial material preparation
- Applied physical science
- Computer literacy
- Basic chemistry
- Basic electronics

Interactive Skills
- Communication with others
- Interpersonal interaction
- Leadership
- Teamwork

Personal Characteristics
- Work orientation
- Adaptability
- Self-confidence
- Stress tolerance

Physical Capabilities
- Strength
- Stamina
- Physical flexibility
- Reaction time
- Whole body steadiness
- Manual dexterity
- Hearing
- Visual acuity
- Visual color perception

Source: Lindquist and Jones, 1992, p. 8. Used by permission of the American Society for Training and Development.

Step 2: Specify Minimum Entry-Level Criteria

Using the list of knowledge, skills, and attitudes on the candidate profile, specify the minimum knowledge, skills, and attitudes that successful applicants must possess when hired, transferred, or promoted. Minimum entry-level criteria make clear precisely what knowledge, skills, and attitudes are most important for successful applicants to bring to the job.

Step 3: Develop Assessment Methods

Develop methods to assess how well each job applicant matches up to the minimum entry-level criteria, based on the applicant's education, training, and work experience. A checklist developed from the job candidate profile will ensure that, during the selection process, interviews (or other selection methods) will compare each applicant's skills directly to the required minimum entry-level criteria for the essential job functions. Then assign a weight to each area of knowledge, skill, or attitude, based on its relative importance to successful job performance.

Step 4: Develop Selection Methods

Using the checklist and profile along with information about each job applicant, develop nondiscriminatory employment interview questions and written or performance-based examinations to compare what applicants know or can do to what they must know or do to perform essential job functions.

Step 5: Use Selection Methods

Use employee selection procedures in conformance with fair employment practices. Screen résumés, employment applications, job posting applications, and other information about applicants. Compare individuals' knowledge and skill to the job-related requirements listed on the profile of the ideal applicant. Through this screening process, narrow the applicant list to three or four finalists, then bring them on-site for multiple interviews, performance tests, and other job-related, nondiscriminatory assessment methods. (Of course, online software can help with screening. But it is not foolproof.) Of growing importance is the use of competency-based selection methods as part of an integrated (and reinvented) HR strategy (Dubois & Rothwell, 2004). However, competency-based methods are not foolproof, either (Carroll & McCrackin, 1998).

Step 6: Select Applicant

Select the most qualified applicant based on his or her previous track record of accomplishments as they relate to minimum entry-level requirements.

Step 7: Discover OJT Needs

Work through the first four questions of the procedure for discovering OJT needs (Chapter Five), asking if the individual is new to the organization, division or department, work unit, or job. If the successful candidate is entering the organization, division, department, or work unit for the first time, orient him or her to the work context. See that the newcomer is provided with peer mentors to ease the transition from the outside and make him or her feel welcome. If the person is new to the job, show the person the current job description and ask him or her to describe previous education, training, or work experience that relates directly to each job function.

Step 8: Compare the Newcomer's Skills to Job Functions

Set the newcomer at ease. Then use the results from the selection process to compare what the person already knows or can do to what he or she must know or do to perform the job competently. Begin the comparison by asking such questions as these:

- What do you already know about how to perform the essential job functions as they are listed on the current job description?
- Explain how you know what you think you know.
- How well do you feel you could recognize appropriate occasions to perform each essential job function?
- For each essential function listed on the job description, tell me your opinions as to why it is important. What consequences do you feel will result from this work?
- For each essential function listed on the job description, tell me what tools or equipment you must possess to carry out the function.
- What do you know already about the job performance standards associated with each function? How do you know about them?
- In your opinion, what are your greatest strengths and weaknesses as they relate to the functions listed on the job description? What do you feel you can do best?
- What makes you think you can perform these functions? In what areas do you need to learn more? Why? What functions are you most interested in? Why?
- How do you learn best? Think of a time when you were very successful in learning a new activity. Describe the situation. Then tell me why, in your opinion, you were especially successful in that experience.

These questions are best asked early in the individual's job tenure so that you can use the answers when preparing a training plan and schedule. If these questions have been posed in preemployment interviews, you can review the answers at this time in order to use them when planning the newcomer's OJT.

Step 9: Prepare OJT Plan and Schedule

Use the results of Steps 1 through 8 when preparing OJT so that the training will focus only on what each individual must know or do to perform effectively. Skip training in job functions that individuals already know or show evidence of being able to do. Of course, knowledge or skill that newcomers claim to have but that cannot be verified should be treated cautiously, and newcomers should usually be asked to demonstrate any area of knowledge or skill before it is accepted as verified.

New Developments in Worker Analysis

It is worth noting at this point that many organizations have been experimenting with competencies and competency models as supplements to traditional work analysis methods. Competencies, while variously defined, usually focus on the characteristics of those who perform the work (Athey & Orth, 1999). There has been great excitement about competency-based approaches because of the potential for productivity improvement they may have (Dubois & Rothwell, 2000, 2004).

Workplace Analysis

A workplace analysis obtains information about the environment in which specific functions must be carried out if they are to be performed competently. It determines the general workplace conditions that must exist, the tools and equipment required, the information the worker needs, the degree of job interdependency required, and the health and safety hazards that exist and ways to minimize the risks from those hazards. To conduct workplace analysis for the purposes of planning OJT, use the workplace analysis worksheet shown in Exhibit 6.7.

When you finish the workplace analysis for a specific job, review the results with experienced job incumbents and supervisors and revise your analysis based on their suggestions. The result of this effort will be a workplace analysis that clarifies how the work setting affects performance and that can be used when preparing a plan and schedule to guide OJT. If you need more information about this step, additional workplace conditions are described in Rothwell and Kazanas (2004). Also, some work analysis methods, such as the Position Analysis Questionnaire (PAQ), simultaneously assess job functions and at least some aspects of the working conditions in which those functions are carried out.

EXHIBIT 6.7. WORKPLACE ANALYSIS WORKSHEET.

Job Title: Date:
Analysis performed by:

Directions: Use this worksheet to analyze the environment in which the worker is to perform each essential job function (you will need one worksheet for each job function). Using a current job description, enter the first essential job function on the worksheet and then answer questions 1 through 5 in relation to that job function. Repeat the process for each essential job function on the job description. (If a number of job functions have the same workplace requirements, combine them on one worksheet.)

Description of essential job function:

1. What conditions must exist in the workplace if the worker is to perform competently?

2. What tools or equipment must be supplied so that the worker can perform this essential job function competently?

3. What information must the worker have access to if the worker is to perform competently?

4. How much interdependency exists between jobs in a work unit or team, and how is team spirit fostered when essential job functions are interdependent?

5. What health and safety hazards are workers exposed to while performing this essential job function, and how can the risks posed by these hazards be minimized?

Supervisor	Date

Trainer	Date

Experienced job incumbent	Date

Summary

This chapter was focused on the second step of the DAPPER model—that is, analyzing the work, worker, and workplace. Planned OJT should be solidly based on what workers are expected to do. It should also take into account their individual capabilities and the conditions of the work environment in which they will perform. In the next chapter we examine how to prepare the training plan. That is, of course, the third step in the DAPPER model.

CHAPTER SEVEN

PREPARING THE TRAINING PLAN

How to Develop the Right Sequence of Activities

Once you have discovered your organization's on-the-job training needs and analyzed the work, workers, and workplace, you are ready to prepare the OJT.

Steps for Preparing OJT

The six steps for preparing OJT consist of reviewing the results of the work, worker, and workplace analyses; preparing performance objectives based on individual learning needs; establishing the means to assess learner mastery; sequencing job functions to be covered in OJT; preparing a plan and schedule to guide OJT; and reviewing the plan and schedule with the learners. After completing these steps, you will prepare the instructional materials to support OJT. This chapter discusses both the six steps and the preparation of the instructional materials.

Step 1: Review Results of the Work, Worker, and Workplace Analyses

Preparation for OJT begins with a review of the results of work, worker, and workplace analyses. Use the results of these analyses to get a big-picture view of the essential job functions on which the learners need to be trained. Be sure that learners have been oriented to the organization, division, department, and/or work unit before OJT starts, so that they understand how the results of their work contribute to the organization's ability to meet its goals and customer needs. Encourage learners' socialization by assigning peer sponsors to them before OJT begins.

Step 2: Prepare Performance Objectives

Develop performance objectives directly from the essential job functions listed on the job description. For each essential function, ask *What should the learner be able to do after training?* Develop at least one terminal performance objective from your answer; then prepare a worksheet on which you can list the essential job functions and their corresponding performance objectives to guide your OJT planning. As Mager (1997) has explained, these objectives should contain descriptions of performance (What will the learner be doing?), conditions (What conditions are assumed to exist during performance?), and criteria (How will performance be identified and measured?). Descriptions of OJT performance objectives should match up with the essential job functions. Conditions should be tied to the results of workplace analysis, indicating the tools, equipment, or other resources with which the learner must be supplied to perform. Criteria should correspond to measurable job performance standards. Although it is possible to express performance objectives in terms of desired final OJT results–typically, the performance level of an experienced worker performing at a normal pace–some OJT trainers prefer to establish weekly, monthly, or bimonthly performance objectives. Such intermediate objectives are a better reflection of the learning curve through which inexperienced performers will progress as they gradually achieve acceptable job performance standards.

Step 3: Establish Means to Assess Learner Mastery

Organizations are often reluctant to use paper-and-pencil testing to assess learner mastery of essential job functions during OJT. Written tests require workers to take time away from their work, time that many supervisors and on-the-job trainers do not have to spare. Also, supervisors and on-the-job trainers should be sensitive to workers' test anxiety (stemming from previous negative testing experiences) and may want to avoid the complaints and questions that stem from that anxiety.

Consequently, alternatives to paper-and-pencil testing must usually be found if trainers are to discover how well the learners are progressing. For example, trainers can pose oral questions to learners during OJT, and the answers can give trainers an immediate indication of how well learners understand what they are doing—and why. Trainers can also give homework or independent study assignments both to reinforce the training and to assess learner mastery, or they can assess the results of the training through the learners' work, checking it against measurable job performance standards or standards for product or service quality. If a team is involved, action learning may be used to ensure some cross-fertilization among members of a group (Rothwell, 1999). Of course, various online testing methods can be used to support OJT (see "Assess, Yes," 2000).

Step 4: Sequence OJT Functions

To be successful, OJT should be organized around learner needs. It should not be sequenced around the daily crises encountered in the work environment. Nor should its sequence be based solely on trainer convenience or learner interests. Job functions affecting worker health and safety should usually be treated first; those affecting more frequently performed activities may be treated next; those most critical to successful performance—or those most prone to missteps—should be prioritized and treated as learners have sufficient knowledge to grasp them. Within this larger frame, essential job functions may be taught in the order in which they should be performed or some order appropriate for a novice in the job. The patterns in which job functions may be appropriately sequenced for OJT are chronological, topical, whole-to-part, part-to-whole, known-to-unknown, or unknown-to-known (Rothwell & Kazanas, 2004).

Chronological Sequencing. To plan chronological, or time-based, sequencing, ask experienced performers to describe the chronological arrangement of the activities necessary to carry out an essential job function and to describe time-based performance cues, such as the day of the week or month or the hour of the day that cues various activities. Use the description to sequence the training.

Topical Sequencing. To use topics as a basis for sequencing, ask experienced performers to clarify the order in which functions should be taught based on the topics the novice performer will need to understand. What topics must be understood before others? Can the material to be taught be sorted into a learning hierarchy in which basic terms are treated first, rudimentary topics or subjects are treated next, and complex topics are treated last? If it can, then you can use the experienced performers' clarification to sequence the learning.

Whole-to-Part Sequencing. Is it possible to develop a model of an entire process and show the relationship of all the job functions that are performed? If the answer is yes, then it may be possible to use whole-to-part sequencing as your OJT organizing scheme. Once again, ask one or more experienced performers to describe the order in which essential job functions should be performed and use the description to construct a model, or simplified representation, around which you can plan the OJT.

Part-to-Whole Sequencing. Is it possible to reverse whole-to-part sequencing? In other words, can you devise a model from an examination of discrete essential job functions? If the answer is yes, then you can employ part-to-whole sequencing, using job activities as the building blocks that will eventually reveal a job function to the novice. You will construct your model from experienced performers' descriptions of the essential functions and their order.

Known-to-Unknown Sequencing. What do the learners already know about an essential function at the time they begin to learn about it? That is the central question to be asked in devising known-to-unknown sequencing, which moves from what learners already know, such as basic terms or tasks, to what they do not know. To sequence tasks from known-to-unknown, share a list of activities (taken from experienced performers' descriptions) with inexperienced performers, asking what they do and do not understand. List what the newcomers do and do not know, show that list to experienced performers, and ask for their help in developing a sequence in which the newcomers can be gradually introduced to the activities they do not know.

Unknown-to-Known Sequencing. Use unknown-to-known sequencing with otherwise experienced learners who are to be retrained. This approach motivates these learners by letting them discover that they are not as knowledgeable as they may have thought. To apply this approach, reverse the procedure for known-to-unknown sequencing. Begin your list of essential functions with what most learners do not know, followed by what they do, and use the list to develop a problem, case study, or other test of knowledge to be shared with learners at the outset of OJT. When they express confusion or difficulty, return to known-to-unknown sequencing.

Step 5: Prepare a Plan and Schedule

Once essential job functions have been sequenced for OJT, prepare a training plan (what training will be conducted) and schedule (when training will be delivered) to guide OJT. A simple way to go about this process is to write training activities and schedules directly on learners' job descriptions. Both one-on-one and large- and small-group training can be noted and scheduled on individuals' job descriptions. As an alternative to indicating when OJT will be scheduled, some trainers note the deadlines for OJT completion. In that way, they can track that training has been delivered or that learners have achieved competency by a certain time.

Step 6: Review Plan and Schedule with Learners

However the OJT plan and schedule are established, they should be reviewed with learners to secure learners' ownership. If the learners have questions at this point, trainers should answer them and allow the learners to suggest justifiable changes.

Designing Instructional Materials

Much has been written about instructional materials—and some of it is unusual, such as those who recommend developing comic books to present OJT (Hartley & Stroupe, 1995). However, most of this literature assumes the training will be presented to a group or, more recently, online. Relatively little has been published on designing instructional materials for one-on-one OJT, drawing directly on materials immediately available in the workplace as content. The authors' year 2003 survey shed some light on what materials, tools, and aids are used to support OJT. (See Figure 7.1.) Approaches that are particularly appropriate for one-on-one on-the-job are described in the following sections.

Topical Outlines

A topical outline summarizes the OJT content and is based on the work, worker, and workplace analyses. It notes what topics will be covered and when they will be presented, although usually not how they will be presented. Topical outlines to guide one-on-one OJT are developed in the same way as outlines for group instruction (Rothwell & Sredl, 2000).

Topical outlines are advantageous for several reasons. First, they can be developed in short order by a subject-matter expert (SME), a characteristic that makes them especially appealing to on-the-job trainers in any organization in which many employees are overloaded with tasks. Second, topical outlines ensure a logical OJT sequence, since the process of preparing them usually requires the writer to think through the logic of the presentation. Third, they can be easily distributed to other trainers and subject-matter experts, who can critique them for completeness and offer suggestions to improve them. Fourth, they can improve the consistency of the one-on-one OJT offered to the various learners of a particular job. Trainers' consistent use of such outlines with all learners may also be sufficient to protect the organization against charges of unfair discrimination in training practices.

FIGURE 7.1. WHAT TOOLS, METHODS, AND AIDS ARE USED TO CONDUCT OJT IN YOUR ORGANIZATION?

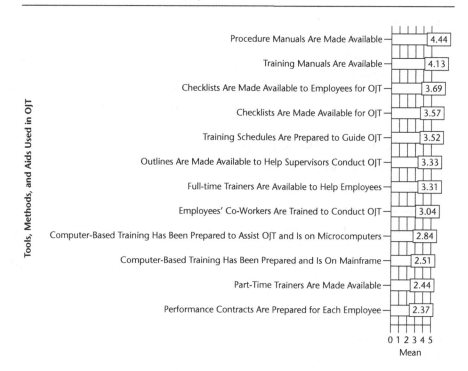

Checklists

A checklist of items allows those items to be confirmed. A job-training checklist may be developed to guide all phases of an individual's OJT. Alternatively, separate task-training checklists may be developed for each essential job function on which individuals are to receive OJT. A job-training checklist (see Exhibit 7.1) should list essential job functions, specify who will receive the training in them and why the training is important, and describe the training kind, methods, schedule or deadline, location (on-the-job, near-the-job, and/or off-the-job), and standards for assessing how well the learners are performing and for giving feedback to the learners about their performance in training on each job function. The checklist should, of course, be consistent with the results of work, worker, and workplace analysis.

The task-training checklist (Exhibit 7.2) covers specific parts of functions that learners will learn, when training will occur, how it will occur, and how task/activity competence or completion of training will be verified.

EXHIBIT 7.1. JOB TRAINING CHECKLIST.

Job Title: Date:
Trainer's Name:
Who will receive OJT?
When will OJT begin?
Why is OJT important?
   New employee   New procedure
   Job change   Other: please describe
   New equipment

1. What function-related training is to be given?

2. What will the training content be? (List it in outline form.)

3. When is the training to be delivered (or by what deadline)?

4. How is training to be given (methods or processes)?

5. How well should the learner perform when the training is complete and how will
   performance be measured?

6. How will feedback be given to the learner about his or her training performance?

Trainer	Date

Learner	Date

We certify that the training plan and schedule have been completed.

Trainer	Date

Learner	Date

Mastering the Instructional Design Process: A Systematic Approach, Third Edition. Copyright © 2004 by
John Wiley & Sons, Inc. Reproduced by permission of Pfeiffer, an Imprint of Wiley. www.pfeiffer.com

Lesson Plans

A lesson plan summarizes who will receive the instruction, what they will learn,
where the lesson will be conducted, why it is important, and how they will
learn it. A lesson plan also covers how learners will be assessed on what
they learned to ensure that they can apply it.

You can write a lesson plan suitable for OJT directly from a current job
description or task analysis. In addition to describing the training itself, it is

EXHIBIT 7.2 TASK TRAINING CHECKLIST.

Job Title: Date:

Trainer's Name:

Who will receive OJT?

When will OJT begin?

Why is OJT important?

___ New employee   ___ New procedure

___ Job change   ___ Other: please describe

___ New equipment

1. What is the job task on which OTJ will be given?

2. What is the training schedule?

3. When is the training strategy?

We verify that the learner has mastered the task: yes   no

Trainer's initials:

Learner's initials:

We certify that the training plan and schedule have been reviewed.

Trainer	Date
Learner	Date

We certify that the training plan and schedule have been completed.

Trainer	Date
Learner	Date

Mastering the Instructional Design Process: A Systematic Approach, Third Edition. Copyright © 2004 by John Wiley & Sons, Inc. Reproduced by permission of Pfeiffer, an Imprint of Wiley. www.pfeiffer.com

important to specify objectives, needed materials, the way the lesson complements other training, and the date the lesson plan was completed. A lesson plan worksheet appears in Exhibit 7.3. Of course, alternative plan formats may be used.

Inquiry Instructional Learning Plans

Kapfer and Kapfer (1978), in what might be regarded as a classic treatment, define an *inquiry instructional learning plan* (ILP) as a means to "bring subject matter

EXHIBIT 7.3. OJT LESSON PLAN WORKSHEET.

Job Title: Date:

Learner's Name:

Trainer's Name:

Why is OJT being conducted now? (Provide reasons.)

1. What are the training objectives (what should the learner be able to do upon completion of training)?

2. What materials, equipment, tools, or other resources are necessary to conduct training?

3. How does this lesson connect to or fit in with other training, and why is this lesson important?

4. What training will be presented, and how it will be presented?

5. How will the learner's mastery be assessed or verified?

Trainer's Notes:

Approvals:

We certify that planned OJT has been completed.

Trainer   Date

Learner   Date

Mastering the Instructional Design Process: A Systematic Approach, Third Edition. Copyright © 2004 by John Wiley & Sons, Inc. Reproduced by permission of Pfeiffer, an Imprint of Wiley. www.pfeiffer.com

content and learning resources together for the learner. Thus, an ILP is not a learning resource in itself; it is an organizer" (p. 3). The knowledge and skills resources toward which an ILP can direct learners, Kapfer and Kapfer explain, "include (1) human resources such as faculty, peers, students, clients, and patients; (2) realia such as artifacts, models, and natural phenomena; and (3) media, including both print and non-print formats" (p. 3). Inquiry ILPs fall into two categories: exploration ILPs and competence ILPs. An *exploration ILP* directs learners to investigate something new through an open-ended inquiry process. The outcomes are not always stated or clear. In contrast, a *competence ILP* directs learners through the process of mastering an activity that they can subsequently do or demonstrate, and the outcomes are specified in advance.

To develop outlines for these ILPs, on-the-job trainers can follow the formats suggested by Kapfer and Kapfer. For an exploration ILP, list or describe the object or event to be investigated, list inquiry questions, specify learning activities and resources, and ask for a summary of what was learned. For a competence ILP, describe the competency to be acquired by the learner, describe or outline the subject matter of the function in which competency is to be acquired, specify learning activities and resources, and establish a means by which to test or assess competency. Exhibit 7.4 illustrates a sample exploration ILP for a simple task, answering a business phone, and Exhibit 7.5 illustrates a competence ILP for another simple task, removing an automobile gas cap. ILPs prepared for OJT will usually be longer than the examples shown because the functions they cover will usually be more complex.

EXHIBIT 7.4. SAMPLE EXPLORATION INQUIRY ILP.

Learner's Name: Date Prepared:

Job Coach: Date Completed:

Object or Event:

Answering a telephone

Inquiry Questions:

1. You may be accustomed to answering the telephone formally at home. But organizations usually require more formality from individuals who answer phones. What are the policies of this organization on answering the phone? Why are these policies established?

Notes:

2. How do people actually answer the phone in this organization? How well does what they do match up to the organization's policies?

Notes:

Learning Activies and Resources

1. Ask your supervisor for copies of any relevant policies on answering the phone.

2. Observe three employees answering the phone in the course of their daily work activities. Note what they do. Compare it to the organization's policy, noting any differences.

3. Ask two co-workers and your supervisor for their opinions about the most common complaints and compliments that customers make about the way employees answer the phone.

Student summary of learning:

Write some notes about what you learned from this investigation. Mention other areas worthy of future investigation. Be prepared to discuss these notes with your trainer.

Mastering the Instructional Design Process: A Systematic Approach, Third Edition. Copyright © 2004 by John Wiley & Sons, Inc. Reproduced by permission of Pfeiffer, an Imprint of Wiley. www.pfeiffer.com

EXHIBIT 7.5. SAMPLE COMPETENCE INQUIRY ILP.

Learner's Name: Date Prepared:

Trainer's Name: Date Completed:

Competence:
Removing a gas cap on an automobile

Description/Outline

1. Familiarize yourself with a gas cap and an automobile. Find examples to examine.

2. Steps in removing a gas cap:
   a. Locate the gas cap on the automobile.
   b. Open the gas cap cover, exposing the gas cap to view.
   c. Turn the gas cap counterclockwise until it comes off.
      Troubleshooting: If the gas cap does not move, push down and then twist. Some gas caps require downward pressure first.
      Troubleshooting: If the gas cap has a key hole, find key and insert it before completing steps a through c. Some gas caps are locked on.
   d. Place gas cap in a secure location once it is removed.

Learning Activities/Resources:

1. Ask experienced co-workers to help you find relevant equipment manuals describing gas caps and removal procedures.

2. Ask a supervisor or co-worker to demonstrate how to remove a gas cap.

3. Ask a supervisor or co-worker to show you the automobiles most commonly used by the organization so that the most frequent gas cap removal activities will be clear to you.

4. Ask experienced co-workers about the most common problems they have encountered when removing gas caps, and what they do to address those problems.

Test:

1. When you have researched gas cap removal and have practiced the procedure, arrange a time to demonstrate what you know to your trainer.

2. Ask your trainer for feedback on your demonstration once it is completed.

Mastering the Instructional Design Process: A Systematic Approach, Third Edition. Copyright © 2004 by John Wiley & Sons, Inc. Reproduced by permission of Pfeiffer, an Imprint of Wiley. www.pfeiffer.com

Learning Contracts

A *learning contract* is a binding agreement about learning between trainers/organizations and learners/individuals. Usually expressed in writing, it is negotiated between trainers and learners or between supervisors and workers and states the results to be achieved through planned learning. Such terms as individual development plan (IDP), learning agreement, learning plan, study plan, and self-development plan are often synonymous with learning contract. In one sense, a learning contract is the mirror image of the job- or task-training checklist because it places the responsibility both for planning OJT and for learning squarely on the learner rather than on the trainer. Instead of directing the learner through OJT activities according to a trainer-prepared schedule, the trainer facilitates the learner's learning process by suggesting sources of job-related information and skill-building activities to the learner. Thus, the trainer functions as a gatekeeper for the learner's networking and as a guide for the learner's self-directed inquiry.

In recent years, individual development plans (IDPs) have enjoyed growing popularity as many organizations adopt succession management efforts that rely on competency models (which describe what kind of person the successful performer should be), 360-degree assessments (which measure individuals against the models), and IDPs to close developmental gaps (see Dubois & Rothwell, 2000, 2004). IDPs contain all the elements of a learning contract, including some method of holding people accountable for results. Many software packages are available to support them—and help the organization inventory the talent available.

As Malcolm Knowles (1986) observes in a classic description: "A learning contract typically specifies (1) the knowledge, skills, attitudes, and values to be acquired by the learner (learning objectives), (2) how these objectives are to be accomplished (learning resources and strategies), (3) the target date for their accomplishment, (4) what evidence will be presented to demonstrate that the objectives have been accomplished, and (5) how this evidence will be judged or validated" (p. 38). Moreover, "contract learning is an alternative way of structuring a learning experience: It replaces a content plan with a process plan. Instead of specifying how a body of content will be transmitted (content plan), it specifies how a body of content will be acquired by the learner (process plan)" (pp. 39–40).

Implementing contract learning in an organization as part of OJT requires leadership. Often that leadership will come from training professionals who educate line managers about the value of learning contracts. However, when moving from traditional (directive) OJT to contract (facilitative) learning, training professionals should take care to emphasize that work, worker, or workplace analysis should not be neglected. Instead, much of the responsibility for those activities should be turned over to the workers themselves, thereby increasing employee involvement and empowerment. Additional steps in applying contract learning include using job descriptions as guides for what is to be learned, expressing the learning contract in writing to clarify key responsibilities of learners and job coaches, advising learners how to get started, and providing learners with concrete and timely feedback so they know how well they are progressing. Exhibit 7.6 contains a learning contract worksheet suitable for use in OJT.

There are four distinct advantages to using learning contracts for OJT rather than more directive methods: (1) as mentioned, responsibility for learning is

EXHIBIT 7.6. LEARNING CONTRACT WORKSHEET.

Job Title: Date:

Learner's Name:

Trainer's Name:

1. What are the objectives?

2. What are the resources/strategies for achieving the objectives?

3. What are the target completion dates for the objectives?

4. What evidence will show mastery?

5. How will this evidence be assessed?

Approvals:

We certify that the training plan and schedule have been reviewed.

Trainer	Date
Learner	Date

We certify that the training plan and schedule have been completed.

Trainer	Date
Learner	Date

Mastering the Instructional Design Process: A Systematic Approach, Third Edition. Copyright © 2004 by John Wiley & Sons, Inc. Reproduced by permission of Pfeiffer, an Imprint of Wiley. www.pfeiffer.com

placed squarely on learners rather than shouldered by trainers; (2) learner dependency on the trainer is decreased and learner empowerment is increased, because learners take an active role in designing and carrying out their own OJT; (3) learners are encouraged to reflect on what they learn as they learn, thereby increasing their opportunities for learning how to learn and for double-loop learning, in which reflection follows action; and (4) less direct supervision of learners is required since learners are encouraged to work on their own. There are also two disadvantages, however, in using learning contracts for OJT. First, trainers may have difficulty adjusting to a new role and may need instruction on negotiating learning contracts, holding learners accountable for results, and functioning as resource and enabling agents. Second, learners may not be comfortable with their new role and may need to be briefed on what contract learning is, what their responsibilities are, why contract learning is advantageous, and how to find information or establish projects to build their own repertoire of knowledge and skills.

Learner Interview Guides

A *learner interview guide* is a list of questions about job functions or tasks. It should be given to newcomers early in their job tenure to guide them through a self-directed inquiry process as a means of performing OJT. Less detailed than an inquiry ILP, an interview guide may be either job comprehensive or task specific. A *job comprehensive learner interview guide* poses questions about all essential job functions for learners to answer; a *task specific learner interview guide* poses questions about tasks related to an essential job function.

A learner interview guide may be thought of as a mirror image of a lesson plan. The lesson plan guides trainers in showing the ropes to a newcomer; the interview guide lists questions that guide newcomers to learn the ropes for themselves and to take personal responsibility for seeking out information and people. An interview guide, however, is typically less detailed than a lesson plan. It provides learners with questions to answer about job functions or tasks but does not offer suggestions about how to answer them. Learners who take the initiative to learn are most likely to succeed with this approach. An added benefit is that this approach sends the message that individuals bear the most responsibility for their own learning and should become competent in doing that (Rothwell, 2002).

To develop an interview guide for use in OJT, subject-matter experts should pool their knowledge. After updating the job description and completing work, worker, and workplace analyses, they should formulate interview guide questions that will lead learners in pursuit of information about their job functions in an organized sequence. They should also encourage learners to take notes as answers to questions are learned, and they should meet periodically with learners to check progress and offer advice about how to obtain the best answers. Interview guides require little time to develop and update, and that is a distinct advantage. However, they may also encourage on-the-job trainers to make training a sink-or-swim venture, and that can be a possible disadvantage. Exhibit 7.7 depicts an interview guide worksheet.

Reading Lists

Most workers are faced with a daily avalanche of memos, letters, reports, electronic mail, voice mail, and fax messages. (The advent of wireless communication is likely to intensify this problem, since wireless makes it possible to reach people in real time–and interrupt whatever they are doing.) Without a means

EXHIBIT 7.7. INTERVIEW
GUIDE WORKSHEET.

Job Title: Date:

Learner's Name:

Trainer's Name:

List essential function from job description:

Answer the following questions about the function:

1. What policies and procedures exist on this issue?

2. What are the recommended procedures?

3. Who performs this function most often? Why?

4. When is the function likely to occur most often?

5. Where (in what parts of the organization) is this function performed most?

6. Why is this function important?

7. How do experienced employees in the job perform this function?

8. Other questions (fill in additional questions as needed):

to organize this and other material for quick reference, they find it difficult to access information when they need it. They may never learn about important organizational policies and procedures until they violate a policy. Lists of reading material can be designed that organize the written references to which workers need to refer as they perform. Job-related reading lists may simply list titles, sources, and other bibliographic information, or they may supply content descriptions of the items. The items themselves might include policy or procedure manuals, memos, letters, forms, newsletter articles, special brochures, equipment manuals, training manuals, and/or electronic mail messages. Reading lists may also consist of references to specific policies and procedures or to the table of contents of a team-based work performance manual or a sourcebook that contains all the key documents in one place. Workers can then go to a central information source as necessary.

To prepare a reading list suitable for OJT, assemble a face-to-face or virtual panel of subject-matter experts, including experienced workers, supervisors, and labor representatives. Show them the job descriptions of all employees in a work unit. Then ask them to identify and organize the important reading material that should be available to these employees. One way for panel members to go about this task is to work through each essential job function listed on the job descriptions. In that way, they can key the reference materials they suggest to essential job functions. Reference materials applicable to more than one function can be cross-referenced. The final reading list will then be based on the panel's findings. Alternatively, a committee of seasoned workers may be asked to identify the most common or most difficult problems they have encountered on their jobs. The critical incident method is used to surface these problems. Then a reading list is created that provides guidance in solving these particularly common or especially difficult job-related problems. Exhibit 7.8 is a worksheet learners can use to identify information appropriate for a reading list. By doing that, learners are also encouraged to take initiative to organize their own learning events.

EXHIBIT 7.8. WORKSHEET FOR DEVELOPING A READING LIST.

Directions: To identify appropriate written references to help you perform essential job functions listed on your current job description, complete a separate reading list worksheet for each essential function listed on your current job description. Follow these steps: (1) find an experienced co-worker, supervisor, or other person who is knowledgeable about the function to be discussed (if you are unsure whether the person is knowledgeable about the function, ask first); (2) arrange a time when you can meet with him or her to ask the questions on this worksheet; (3) record your notes on the answers; (4) arrange a time for a debriefing with your trainer about the answers you receive. (You may wish to ask a person about several essential functions at once, but we advise against your asking one person about more than three.)

Learner's Name: Job Title: Date of Interview:

Person Interviewed:

Essential Function:

1. Tell me a story about [describe essential function]. What is the single most difficult situation *you have faced in your experience* in performing this function? Describe the situation.

2. What did you do in that situation, and why?

3. Suppose you faced the same situation again. How would you handle it, and why?

4. What advice can you give me about the right kinds of references that I could review to help me address the kind of problem you described?

5. What other advice do you have for me? Why do you provide this particular advice?

Reading lists and job reference manuals should be periodically reviewed and updated on a scheduled basis. If all employees have access to electronic mail, a reading list such as the table of contents of a performance manual can be stored electronically for easy access. To use a reading list for OJT, give the appropriate list to newcomers, asking them to review the policies or procedures applicable to a function on which they will receive instruction. Ambitious learners can be encouraged to pose questions about how to improve existing policies and procedures. In that way, the organization harnesses the objectivity of newcomers, who are not blinded by the organization's culture, "the way things have always been done here."

A key advantage of reading lists is that they are a source of continuing job performance guidance for newcomers and veterans alike. A key disadvantage is that a number of workers may be less inclined to read about how to solve problems than to ask others about appropriate solutions. Asking others can pose a distraction, but it can also be an effective way to learn new information.

A computer-based referencing system (CBR) is a technologically assisted version of a reading list—only it is more focused. A CBR places all organizational documents on a database that can be accessed in real time. Using a CBR, a performer can access all organizational documents and search by keyword to find relevant information. Such a system, if it exists in the organization, should be emphasized to real-time learners, since it can place much information directly at their fingertips when they need it.

Document and Case Reviews

Document and case reviews are common methods of training newcomers on the job. When document reviews are used, newcomers are asked to read job-related material to familiarize themselves with job functions and the organization, division, department, and/or the work unit. For example, they may be asked to read the company's annual report. In a case review, newcomers are asked to retrace the steps of an actual work case or tricky problem situation that has been either successfully or unsuccessfully handled. Taken together, document and case reviews are powerful methods for OJT because they actively engage learners in real-life problems and situations. They are also a means by which to preserve institutional memory about what works and what does not work.

To prepare a document review suitable for OJT, assemble a panel of experienced workers who are familiar with the job-related references to which they must refer during their work and ask panel members to identify this appropriate, important job-related reading material. Prepare a packet of these documents or forms to share with newcomers as part of their OJT.

Use a similar approach to set up case reviews. Assemble a face-to-face or virtual panel of experienced workers and ask them to identify specific critical work situations they have encountered. If a case has a paper trail, such as letters or other information, assemble the documents chronologically so that the new workers can review case events as they unfolded. When you share the case with newcomers, explain what objectives are to be achieved through the case review and how the case pertains to the workers' essential job functions. After workers have read through the case file but before they learn how the case was actually handled, ask them for their conclusions and recommendations for action. Use this discussion to coach and tutor the learners on the most important issues in the case and how these issues bear on the learners' essential job functions.

Document reviews are advantageous in OJT because they emphasize key printed resources about which newcomers should be aware; a key disadvantage is that they require time to assemble. Case reviews are advantageous because they provide information in a realistic, engaging, and job-related context. Here, a key disadvantage is that learners, who are usually not called on to demonstrate behavior while reviewing a case, may not fully appreciate the case's importance or its implications for job performance until they have acquired hands-on experience in the job.

Summary

In this chapter we focused on the third step of the DAPPER model—that is, preparing the training plan to guide OJT. As we pointed out, preparing the training plan can be accomplished in six steps: (1) review results of the work, worker, and workplace analyses; (2) prepare performance objectives; (3) establish means to assess learner mastery; (4) sequence OJT functions; (5) prepare a plan and schedule; and (6) review plan and schedule with learners. In the next chapter we examine how to present OJT, which is the fourth step in the DAPPER model.

CHAPTER EIGHT

PRESENTING THE TRAINING

How to Conduct the OJT Session

After preparing your planned on-the-job training, turn to the fourth step of the DAPPER model–*presenting OJT.* In this chapter we address desirable characteristics of on-the-job trainers and learners and the steps trainers should take in presenting OJT.

Desirable Characteristics of Trainers and Learners

Individual responsibility for OJT must be clarified, usually through job descriptions and other formal directives. On-the-job trainers and learners alike feel confident about what they are expected to do in OJT and how they will be held accountable for it only when their level of responsibility has been clearly defined. It may be helpful, then, to prepare a job description that describes what on-the-job trainers are supposed to do. A comparable job description can also be prepared for learners. If OJT is offered in a work team context, team members may also be involved in a team-based job description that clarifies what roles should be enacted by co-workers during the OJT process.

The Trainer's Role

On-the-job trainers play three critically important roles in OJT: (1) they provide guidance on proper ways to perform work tasks; (2) they provide social support so learners feel psychologically comfortable; and (3) they model effective role behavior within an organization's corporate culture. Supervisors, even when not serving as on-the-job trainers, bear the responsibility for ensuring that workers receive OJT. It is up to them to juggle work schedules or staffing to make the time and the people available for OJT. Moreover, when accidents or other performance problems are directly traceable to a lack of OJT, the supervisor is usually held accountable.

On-the-job trainers (in addition to whatever other responsibilities they may have as supervisors, co-workers, or training professionals) specifically bear the responsibility for ensuring that one-on-one training sessions embody the following six conditions for change and learning. These six conditions are the same as those classically described as essential in employee counseling (see Rogers, 1967, p. 73):

1. Two people are assigned to work together.
2. The first person (in this case, the learner) feels anxious but motivated in approaching the situation, which will require change through learning.
3. The second person (in this case, the trainer) feels confident of his or her own knowledge, skills, and abilities.
4. The trainer positively and unconditionally accepts the learner for who he or she is.
5. The trainer also empathizes with the learner, understanding how he or she must feel, and communicates this to the learner.
6. The trainer communicates his or her feelings of positive acceptance to the learner.

In addition, effective on-the-job trainers should demonstrate all the skills of effective group facilitators. More specifically, they should be able to do the following in their OJT training sessions:

- Use effective nonverbal behavior to show interest in what learners say or do and to demonstrate that the trainer considers learners (and the training experience) important.
- Listen actively and pay close attention to what learners seem to be feeling as well as to what they say.
- Effectively paraphrase what learners say over short time spans.
- Effectively summarize what learners say over long time spans.
- Observe learners carefully to assess learners' feelings through observation of body language.
- Question learners effectively, using open-ended questions when appropriate to seek information about what is being learned or gain insight about learners' feelings.

- Use closed questions when appropriate to guide conversations and maintain control over time used for OJT.
- Express their own thoughts.
- Express their own feelings.
- Focus learners' attention on one or, at most, a few worthy issues at a time.
- Focus what learners think about an issue.
- Challenge learners to approach problems creatively.

These skills are essentially the same as those required for effective counselors, psychotherapists, organization development practitioners, training group facilitators, and other helping professionals (see Rothwell, 1999). It is possible to establish and implement a certification for on the job trainers (Walter, 1002), a process in which there is growing interest.

Finally, effective on-the-job trainers should have a thorough grasp of adult learning principles. While these principles do not apply to all adults, and it is dangerous to assume that they do, they are effective for teaching many adults. Hence, knowledge of them is important when presenting OJT. It may also be important to be able to adapt OJT to help those with learning disabilities—as dramatized in an interesting case study from the U.K. (Arkin, 1995).

It is worth emphasizing that there is such a thing as a *learning disability,* defined as "a neurological disorder that affects the brain's ability to receive, process, store, and respond to information" (LD at a glance, n.d.).As that website also notes, "individuals with learning disabilities are protected under the Individuals with Disabilities Education Act (IDEA) of 1997 and Americans with Disabilities Act of 1990." More information on learning disabilities can be obtained from Bensimon (1996) and Flynn (1996). In the United States, approximately 2.9 million schoolchildren are thought to have specific learning disabilities, and that number represents about 5 percent of public school students. That may translate into about 5 percent of the workforce.

The Learners' Co-Workers' Role

Learners' co-workers often play critically important roles in delivering or supporting OJT, although their roles are often not considered as important as they really are. While it is widely recognized that co-workers may substitute for supervisors as on-the-job trainers and coaches, it is less widely acknowledged that co-workers shape learners' opinions about work behaviors and results. Therefore, co-workers should, at least, take on these responsibilities:

- Approach newcomers with positive attitudes about the learning task and the work environment.

- Explain not just what to do but also why a particular task or function is important to customers.
- Provide social support during the learning process so as to build learners' confidence.
- Possess sufficient interpersonal skills to conduct OJT when appropriate and preserve learners' self-esteem.
- Take responsibility for the training they offer, realizing that it is as important as the work.
- Serve as positive role models.
- Make few assumptions about what newcomers already know or are able to do.
- Participate in developing an organized OJT plan and schedule so learners can be held accountable for their OJT progress and trainers can be held accountable for the OJT they present.

Other responsibilities could be added to this list. The important point is that the organization must clarify what the responsibilities are for each person who acts to train others, communicate the responsibilities, describe how people will be held accountable for the responsibilities, and continuously monitor results.

The Learner's Role

Individuals receiving OJT bear responsibility that is at least as great as the trainer's. They should, at the least, assume these duties:

- Enter jobs or tasks with positive attitudes.
- Be open to learning.
- Recognize the importance of OJT.
- Enter OJT possessing sufficient basic skills to meet the minimum entry-level job requirements.
- Take responsibility for their own learning.
- Take notes, ask questions, and show interest in what they are learning.
- Expect to learn throughout their careers.
- Encourage a positive and psychologically comfortable climate in which both their own and their co-workers' learning can flourish.
- Provide a positive role model for other learners when appropriate.

Much work in recent years has focused on the learner's role. Gone are the days when learners could be passive, waiting for trainers to tell them what to do. Recent interest has focused around making the work environment more conducive to real-time learning and individual learning competence (Dobbs, 2000; Rothwell, 2002; Seibert, 1999).

Steps Governing OJT Presentation

To deliver effective on-the-job training, those presenting OJT should follow the nine steps described in the following sections.

Step 1: Arrange Work Area

The trainer's first step is to arrange the work area so it is functional for training. On most occasions and for most OJT, the ideal position for trainers and learners is side by side. The trainer should be able to stand or sit next to the learner, and physical barriers, such as desks or work stations, should not prevent the learner from clearly observing work demonstrations. The training plan, which the trainer has prepared beforehand, should specify all equipment, tools, or materials that will be needed (see Exhibits 6.7 and 7.3), and these necessary materials should be placed in the work area before training is conducted. The trainer should also take action to minimize distractions in the work area, arranging for telephone calls to be held and discouraging others from casual visiting during training. In some organizations, in order to deter drop-in visitors, trainers simply place a large "Training in Progress" sign at the work station.

Step 2: Set Learner at Ease

As the second step in OJT, the trainer should set the learner at ease, reducing the learner's anxiety and providing a psychologically supportive climate. Some trainers find it helpful to begin with small talk, which builds rapport, demonstrates personal concern, and communicates friendliness. Some begin a one-on-one training session by telling the learner about the function or task he or she will learn. In this preliminary discussion, the trainer may find it worthwhile to review performance objectives, clarify measurable job performance standards, explain why the job function to be taught is important, and review how the job function relates to other functions (see Exhibits 6.3, 6.7, and 7.1).

Step 3: Show Learner How to Perform

Next, the trainer demonstrates how to perform the job function and how to meet measurable job performance standards or supervisory/customer expectations. The trainer actually shows the learner what to do, often with the learner and trainer standing or sitting side by side. If a decision-making process rather than an observable behavior is to be taught, the trainer may explain the decision steps.

The trainer may also discuss the performance cues that provide guidance about what to do, the ways the learner can recognize these cues in the future, and the exceptions, if any, to the procedures being taught.

Many trainers believe that learners should take notes during this step. Research results do not necessarily support the notion that note taking increases retention (Laird, 1985); however, notes can be useful for future reference. Therefore, trainers may offer guidance to learners about effective note-taking techniques and effective ways to organize information for future use.

Step 4: Explain Key Points

Having demonstrated an essential job function or reviewed the steps in reaching a decision, the trainer should next explain and emphasize key points. To that end, he or she may double-check what the learner knows by posing questions about the job function. Among the important questions for the trainer to ask are the so-called *7-H questions*:

- W*Ho* should perform this function?
- W*Ha*t should be done?
- W*He*n should the function be performed?
- W*He*re should this function be performed, and what tools, equipment, or other support devices should be used?
- W*Hy* should the function be performed? How does the function relate to the work of others? How does it help meet or exceed customer needs?
- *H*ow should the function be performed? Are there policies, procedures, or regulations affecting the way the function is to be performed, or do learners have the discretion to perform the task however they see fit?
- *H*ow is success measured? What are the performance standards affecting the function?

The 7-H questions are depicted in Figure 8.1.

Step 5: Show Learner How to Perform Again

Research on short-term memory suggests that people forget most of what they hear in about forty-eight hours. By demonstrating a function again–essentially, replicating Step 3–trainers increase the odds that what they demonstrate will stick. For this reason, it is desirable for trainers to reenact demonstrations or review the steps in reaching a decision. Learner retention can also be increased

FIGURE 8.1. THE 7-H QUESTIONS.

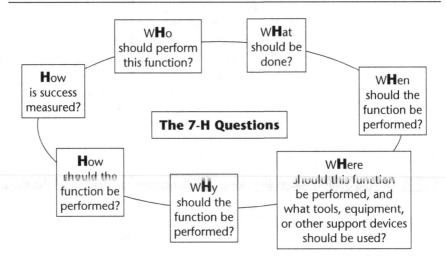

by combining stimuli in order to affect more than one learner sense—sight, hearing, touch, smell, or taste—in that order.

Step 6: Let Learner Do Simple Parts of the Job

Having explained the function or decision-making activity to the learner, the trainer should give the learner a chance to do the activity. Complex activities should be broken down into discrete, manageable parts and the learner should be given a chance to demonstrate the simple parts first. After he or she demonstrates the activity, the learner should receive specific, timely feedback about how well he or she performed. The trainer should offer constructive criticism, praising what was done right and offering suggestions for improvement. Constructive criticism avoids ridicule or sarcasm. It focuses on what should be done more than on what should not be done. The value of feedback in improving individual performance is great and should not be underestimated.

Step 7: Let Learner Perform the Whole Job as Trainer Watches

Once the learner has demonstrated the ability to perform simple parts of a job, he or she can perform the whole job. Over the course of training, learners and trainers essentially switch roles as learners take center stage to perform while trainers sit or stand nearby, observe, and intervene only periodically—often only when learners are experiencing significant performance problems or when they ask for help. In this step, trainers should provide feedback periodically rather than frequently, with hourly, daily, and weekly feedback gradually taking over from more immediate feedback about performance.

Step 8: Let Learner Perform the Whole Job Alone

During Step 8, the trainer gradually fades from the scene, leaving the learner alone to perform the whole job and assume responsibility for it. Trainers who are reluctant to allow workers to function independently risk encouraging time-consuming dependency. They also reinforce the unwillingness of some learners with low self-esteem to assume complete responsibility for what they do. A good approach for trainers at this step in the training process is to establish a random observation schedule, akin to a random reinforcement schedule, in which trainers plan to make visits but perform the planned visits at unpredictable times in order to observe performance or inspect work results.

Step 9: Put Learner on His or Her Own, with Periodic Feedback

At some point the learner should be formally released from training. In some organizations, this release occurs through a formal certification process, a rite of passage that makes clear that learners are now fully responsible for what they do. In this way, the organization, as represented by the trainers, demonstrates confidence that the learners are fully trained to perform all essential job functions in conformance with measurable job performance standards.

Another way to release the learner from training is to ask the on-the-job trainer to prepare a final training progress report (TPR) and state in writing that the learner has completed the training period. The occasion of a TPR also provides the trainer with a valuable opportunity to offer well-deserved praise, give supportive feedback, or establish long-term training objectives, such as cross-training or multiskilling initiatives in which workers learn the job functions and skills of others on a team or in a department.

If the learner does not feel that he or she has been fully trained, or if the learner is not performing in conformance with measurable job performance standards, then that learner should not be released from training. As soon as the problem becomes apparent, the trainer should conduct a fact-finding and problem-solving session to determine the underlying causes of the problem and to reach agreement between the learner and the organization's representatives, including trainer and supervisor, about an appropriate action plan to rectify them. Of course, learners should be actively involved in this problem-solving process, offering any insights they may have about the causes of their performance problems and any ways those causes might be addressed. The solution may involve offering the learner intensive OJT, a refresher on OJT already conducted, or structured practice on selected job functions.

During a problem-solving session, trainers should scrupulously establish a written record that clearly answers the following questions:

- What is happening? (Describe the current situation or performance problem.)
- What should be happening? (Describe measurable job performance standards, supervisory expectations, or customer requirements and provide evidence that they are equitable.)
- Why is the difference important? (Describe the consequences of poor performance to the organization, division, department, or work unit.)
- What appears to be the problem? (Describe the underlying cause, if known.)
- What should the learner do to rectify the problem and thereby succeed in OJT? (The trainer should provide clear, concrete suggestions for improvement.)
- What will happen if performance does not improve? (Specify the next step to be taken if performance does not improve, including any corrective action that will be administered.)
- How much time will the organization allow for improvement? (Provide a date for action that is related to a milestone for performance, but make sure that the learner has sufficient time to demonstrate improvement.)

Generally, trainers should not delay in taking action on OJT performance problems. If, for example, the learner is not progressing in OJT as quickly as past learners have progressed, a fact-finding session should be held as soon as the trainer notices this slower pace.

Summary

In this chapter we focused on presenting the training. Nine key steps were listed in that process: (1) arrange the work area; (2) set the learner at ease; (3) show the learner how to perform; (4) explain the key points; (5) show the learner how to perform again; (6) let the learner do simple parts of the job; (7) let the learner perform the whole job as trainer watches; (8) let the learner perform the whole job alone; and (9) put the learner on his or her own, with periodic feedback. The chapter also described the so-called *7-H question model,* which is relevant to Step 4. The *7-H questions* are: (1) wHo should perform this function? (2) wHat should be done? (3) wHen should the function be performed? (4) wHere should this function be performed, and what tools, equipment, or other support devices should be used? (5) wHy should the function be performed? How does the function relate to the work of others? How does it help meet or exceed customer needs? (6) How should the function be performed? Are there policies, procedures, or regulations affecting the way the function is to be performed, or do learners have the discretion to perform the task however they see fit? and (7) How is success measured?

In the next chapter we turn to the fifth step in the DAPPER model and to evaluating results.

CHAPTER NINE

EVALUATING RESULTS

How to Assess Post-Training Job Performance

Evaluating results is the fifth step of the DAPPER model. If the learner can perform essential job functions in conformance with measurable job performance standards under the trainer's watchful eye, on-the-job training is usually evaluated as successful. Moreover, on-the-job trainers do not face the same daunting challenges that plague efforts to evaluate classroom training: they do not have to worry that peer pressure from supervisors or co-workers will prevent learners from applying what they learned or that the learners will forget what to do in the time between attending a class and performing on the job. In OJT, little or no time lag exists between instruction and application, and supervisors or co-workers typically are the trainers.

Nevertheless, evaluation is, of course, important because it is the means by which training demonstrates the value it adds to the organization. Without evaluation, training may appear to be frivolous, and may thus fall victim to cutbacks during downsizing or restructuring. Moreover, many observers of the training field have complained that organizations devote too little time and too few resources to training evaluation.

OJT and Kirkpatrick's Levels of Evaluation

Donald Kirkpatrick (1997) has developed a scheme to conceptualize training evaluation, identifying four levels of evaluation and arranging them hierarchically from least to most difficult. The lowest and easiest level is evaluation in terms of learner reaction: Did the learners like the training? The second level of evaluation is learning: What was learned from training? The third level is behavior: How much did the learners change their behavior as a result of the training? The fourth level of evaluation, and the most challenging to assess, is results: How much organizational improvement resulted from learners' behavioral changes? These four levels, which are commonly associated with evaluation of group training, also apply to OJT, and in this chapter we discuss how trainers and organizations can use each level with their own OJT.

Level 1: Evaluating Reactions

Unlike classroom activity, OJT is rarely evaluated by attitude surveys (sometimes called smile sheets) administered at the end of a training session to assess how much learners enjoyed the experience or perceived it to be useful to them. One reason end-of-training reactions are rarely checked in OJT is that OJT trainers often have difficulty determining precisely when the end of training occurs. That difficulty can be rectified, of course, by instituting a formal procedure to certify and release learners from OJT (Mueller, 1997). Additionally, because OJT is often conducted one-on-one, there is ample opportunity for trainer and learner to discuss the value of the training experience as it progresses. Unlike classroom training, OJT lends itself to give-and-take between trainer and learner. The trainer can provide prompt, specific feedback; trainer demonstrations can be hands-on; and the trainer can judge the effectiveness of the instructional methods by directly observing what the learner subsequently does and how well. Similarly, the learner's questions can be formulated around actual job problems or situations. The learner's concerns about how he or she is being trained can be directly communicated to the trainer, and the learner can work with the trainer to identify immediate solutions.

Administering Attitude Surveys

Nevertheless, attitude surveys can be used periodically and effectively in OJT. To do so, trainers require only an evaluation instrument covering key issues (see Exhibit 9.1), a willingness to use the instrument, and sufficient trust between trainers and learners to ensure that evaluation questions will be answered truthfully. The evaluation instrument can be administered periodically—say, once a week or once a month—and the results can be the focus of off-the-job problem-solving sessions between the trainer and learner, in which they develop specific corrective action plans. Great care must be taken, however,

EXHIBIT 9.1. OJT REACTION WORKSHEET.

Directions to Trainer: Administer this reaction worksheet periodically during the planned on-the-job training. Establish a regular time for giving it to a learner, such as at the end of a day, once a week, or at the end of each month.

Directions to Learner: Use this reaction worksheet to provide feedback to your trainer and others about the on-the-job training you have received. Read each statement and fill in the blank with the number that you feel most accurately describes your reaction to the statement and your training. After you complete the worksheet, return it to your trainer.

Strongly Agree	Agree	Slightly Agree	Slightly Disagree	Disagree	Strongly Disagree	Neutral
7	6	5	4	3	2	1

Training Purpose, Objectives, and Structure

1. I feel that the trainer effectively explains the plan and schedule for the on-the-job training I am about to receive. _____
2. The trainer effectively explains how each training activity relates to the overall training plan and schedule. _____
3. The trainer effectively states the performance results to be achieved for each function on which I am to be trained. _____

Training Content

4. I feel that the material covered in OJT is important to me in my job. _____

Training Delivery

5. The trainer uses effective methods to meet the training objectives. _____
6. The trainer is effective in presenting information that I must know to do my job in the future. _____
7. The trainer has a good working relationship with me. _____
8. I rarely feel nervous about the training I am receiving. _____
9. My trainer sets a positive example for me to follow. _____
10. I feel free to ask questions of my trainer whenever necessary. _____
11. The trainer frequently tells me why it is important to do what I am being trained to do. _____
12. The trainer frequently shows me how to perform a job task or function. _____
13. The trainer frequently gives me a chance to demonstrate the performance of a job task or function. _____
14. The trainer gives me prompt, specific, and helpful feedback to encourage me to perform in the ways that I am being trained to perform. _____
15. The trainer makes an effort to clarify the job performance standards for each task or function on which I am trained. _____

Use of Time

16. Time is effectively used in my on-the-job training. _____
17. I am being given the proper amount of time to learn my job through the on-the-job training that I am receiving. _____

Overall Evaluations

18. I feel that my on-the-job training is being properly managed. _____

19. What *specific areas for improvement,* if any, do you see in your on-the-job training?

20. What *specific areas are being particularly well-handled* in your on-the-job training, in your opinion?

21. Please add any comments you might wish to make.

      Thank you for your cooperation! *(Please return this evaluation to your trainer.)*

to ensure that learners are not punished in any way for their candor; rather, any complaints they make should be taken only as a signal that joint problem solving is needed.

Typically, however, trainers receive learners' feedback and their reactions to OJT from such sources as conversations and exit questionnaires rather than from reaction surveys.

Holding Conversations with Learners

Conversations about the training should occur throughout OJT. To start such conversations, the trainer needs only to prompt the learner by asking such direct questions as these:

- How much do you like the OJT you have been receiving? (If the learner identifies a problem, the trainer should ask follow-up questions to determine what the problem is and how it may be corrected.)
- How do you feel that I could improve the training methods that I am using? (The phrasing of this question avoids asking the learner for criticism or complaints and, instead, focuses the learner's attention on what trainers could do to improve.)
- How do you feel about the speed of your training? Is the speed too fast, too slow, or about right?
- How effective are the methods that have been used in your on-the-job training so far?

In addition, to use conversations effectively, the trainer can follow these four techniques:

1. Solicit opinions from the learner regularly. A good approach is to check daily with the learner about how he or she feels the OJT is progressing, perhaps at the end of each day spent in OJT.
2. Establish trust and rapport with the learner. Learners may hesitate to speak up to their supervisors or even to experienced co-workers if they fear repercussions. Set the learner at ease and encourage a frank exchange of opinions.
3. Be open-minded. If the learner expresses dissatisfaction with the methods used in OJT, the trainer should be willing to use alternative methods.
4. Be supportive rather than critical. Remember that adults generally learn best in a psychologically supportive environment. Hence, trainers should take active steps to praise learners for what they do right and offer concrete suggestions for improvement when necessary.

Administering Exit Questionnaires

Exit questionnaires are completed by terminating employees and may also be used with employees who are transferring from one work unit or department to another. Exit questionnaires are typically designed to gather information about the reasons for a voluntary separation. They pose such questions as these:

- What was your job title?
- Who was your immediate supervisor?
- How long have you been employed by this organization?
- Are you leaving for a job with another organization? If so, which organization?
- What will you earn in your new job?
- When will you be starting the new job?
- What did you think of your supervisor in this organization?
- How was morale in your work unit?
- How effective was the on-the-job training you received? What could make it more effective for other employees in the future?
- Who was your trainer?

Departing workers' answers to these and other questions can often shed light on ways to improve an organization's OJT practices.

Employees who complete exit questionnaires should be allowed to respond anonymously so that they need not worry that their negative remarks might jeopardize their future requests for work references from the organization. In addition, terminating employees should be told who will see the exit questionnaires, how the results will be used, and how long the questionnaires will remain on file. To derive maximum benefit from exit questionnaires, organizations should use them as a starting point for action planning to improve conditions affecting employees, including the quality of employees' OJT.

Level 2: Evaluating Learning

The evaluation of learning is customarily associated with testing to determine what and how much learners have retained. In classroom training, paper-and-pencil examinations are sometimes used. In OJT, the trainer may evaluate learning informally by giving the learner oral feedback or written notes on learning progress. The trainer may also evaluate learning formally through oral, written, or performance-based examinations.

Trainer Feedback and Notes

As the learner performs functions on which he or she has received OJT, the trainer should observe learner performance, and the information obtained from observation should become the basis for written or oral praise or suggestions for improvement. To provide oral feedback, trainers need only offer timely, specific remarks about learners' performance. In such instances, job performance standards need not be written and used as a point of comparison with worker performance. Indeed, these standards sometimes exist only in trainers' heads, as is true in many small businesses. Written notes about learner performance should usually be more organized than oral feedback. As the learner performs, the trainer observes and take notes about what the learner does, how he or she does it, and how well he or she does it. The notes should compare the learner's performance to measurable standards and should become the basis for feedback. If the learner does not progress satisfactorily, these notes may also become the basis for subsequent corrective action, including disciplinary action when warranted.

Written Examinations

It is difficult to imagine how paper-and-pencil examinations could be effectively administered to learners on their jobs. Would people have to stop working while they took the examinations? While that may be one way to administer written tests, it is not the only way. One alternative is to give learners take-home examinations based on OJT lessons. A second alternative is to ask them to demonstrate what they have learned through performance examinations on the job. A third alternative is to give them frequent, brief quizzes based on bite-sized chunks of instruction delivered on the job.

Test development is an established field of study in its own right. Employers have predictably focused most of their attention on the selection tests that help them identify the individuals who are qualified for particular jobs. In reality, however, an on-the-job training test is also a form of selection test, since continued failure on the test will usually lead to reassignment or even dismissal. Hence, OJT tests, while they should be kept simple, should also comply with the Uniform Guidelines on Employee Selection Procedures (Equal Employment Opportunity Commission, 1978). There are several standard formats for written examinations, including multiple-choice, true/false, matching-item, short-answer, and essay formats. The rest of this section offers examples of these formats and some suggestions for employing the formats successfully. Of course, software is available to support the design of knowledge tests.

Multiple-choice tests require the learner to select the correct answer to a question from a list of answers.

> *Example:* According to company policy, you should do what when answering the phone? (Pick one answer and circle it.)
> (a)   Greet caller, give company name and your name.
> (b)   Say, "Hello."
> (c)   Greet caller, give your name.
> (d)   None of the above.

Multiple-choice tests are appropriate to test the ability of the learner to distinguish the best alternative among several possibilities or to limit successful guessing by learners. Base multiple-choice tests on training material. For each question, write between one and three sentences, called the *question stem,* to introduce the choices. Then identify and write several answers for the learner to choose from (pick several that look right but are not). Administer the test to experienced workers to check its effectiveness, and then revise the test as necessary, correcting unclear wording or clarifying choices provided.

True/false tests ask learners to determine whether a statement is true or not. Alternatively, yes/no or correct/incorrect may also be used as answers.

> *Example:* Two blasts of the company whistle indicate a fire.
> (Circle your answer.)   T   F

True/false tests can only be used for issues that lend themselves to true/false or right/wrong answers. For each test item, write a statement that is clearly true or false and is based on training material. Then check the test's effectiveness and correct it as described for the multiple-choice test.

Matching-item tests require learners to match items drawn from two lists according to some specified relationship.

> *Example:* Match items in Column A to the most appropriate description in Column B. (Draw lines between items to show which ones belong together.)

A	B
Overhead transparencies	Should usually be used in a dark room
Slides	Should usually be used with small groups unless special projection equipment is available
Videotapes	Should be limited to thirty-five letters or less

A matching-item examination can be used to test comprehension, recall, or application. These examinations are especially appropriate for testing learners' knowledge of terms and of the terms' definitions, principles, and applications. For each item, prepare two lists of terms to be matched, making sure there is only one right choice for each matched pair. Then assess the test's effectiveness and revise it if necessary.

Short-answer tests require the learner to fill in a blank with one or several words in order to complete a sentence or series of sentences.

> *Example:* OJT should not be used when learner or co-worker (<u>safety</u>) might be endangered.

Short-answer examinations can test recall, comprehension, or application. For each item, write a sentence or series of sentences based on the training material and then remove a key word or phrase from what you have written. The material that remains should provide a cue that indicates the nature of the word or phrase required. Assess the examination and make necessary changes.

Essay tests ask learners to write long narratives to answer each question.

> *Example:* When should the flange valves on the forging machine be closed? (Describe all the conditions that must be present.)

Essay tests can be used to evaluate learners' abilities to analyze, evaluate, or synthesize information. These tests are prepared by constructing questions about job-related issues, events, and procedures. To grade the response to each question consistently, the person developing the test should also develop a list of the general topics that must be covered for the response to be acceptable. Essay tests, too, must be assessed for effectiveness and revised before they are administered to the learners themselves.

Level 3: Evaluating Behavioral Change

OJT should change what learners do. Thus, the question that is the central focus of behavioral change evaluation is, *How well can the learner carry out essential job functions?* Trainers can evaluate behavioral change through behavioral checklists and performance appraisal.

Behavioral Checklists

Behavioral checklists are developed from task analysis results, and they compare what learners do with what they are expected to do, determining how often learners exhibit desired behaviors or how well they perform the behaviors. Behaviors are listed in sequence of expected occurrence, and trainers simply check off whether the behaviors were exhibited or properly performed by learners. These checklists have the advantages of being quickly developed and easy to use. They also lend themselves well to specific documentation of learner performance. Exhibit 9.2 depicts a sample behavioral checklist.

Performance Appraisals

Most organizations have some system of employee performance appraisal, and in some organizations, those responsible for OJT prefer to use the performance appraisal process to evaluate learning, although training appraisals may also

EXHIBIT 9.2. SAMPLE BEHAVIORAL CHECKLIST.

Learner's Name: Job Title: Date:

Trainer's Name:

Why is OTJ being conducted now?

Is the learner able to:	Has the trainer observed the behavior?		Date and trainer's initials
	Yes	No	
1. Explain the uses of a telephone on the job, emphasizing the most common reasons for which people will call *this* learner in his or her job?	( )	( )	
2. Explain how each function of the phone is used, using phone buttons as the means of organizing the description?	( )	( )	
3. Describe the function of each key on the phone pad?	( )	( )	
4. Demonstrate the proper use of each function for each key on the phone?	( )	( )	

be kept separate from performance appraisals. To use performance appraisal to evaluate learners' OJT performance, on-the-job trainers usually begin by developing an appropriate appraisal form in cooperation with line managers. They may use a committee of intended users to develop the form, if that seems to be the best way to ensure ownership on the part of those users. While it is usually advisable to tie the appraisal directly to essential job functions so that clear, job-related feedback may be provided to learners, that objective may require the time-consuming development of a separate appraisal form for each job. As an alternative, on-the-job trainers may choose to develop an open-ended form (see Exhibit 9.3).

EXHIBIT 9.3. TRAINING PROGRESS REPORT/APPRAISAL WORKSHEET.

Learner's Name:　　　　　　Job Title:　　　　　　Date of Report:

Trainer's Name:

Why is the learner being evaluated now?

Learner Progress	*Rating*		*Trainer's Comments*
	Acceptable	*Unacceptable*	
1. Attendance	( )	( )	
2. Timely arrival at work	( )	( )	
3. Cooperation with co-workers	( )	( )	
4. Progress in training on (list job functions in abbreviated form and rate separately):	( )	( )	

Trainer's overall comments:

Learner's overall comments:

Approvals:

We certify that the training progress report has been completed. The learner's signature below does not necessarily indicate agreement with the report but does indicate that it was conducted.

Trainer	Date
Learner	Date

After developing an appraisal form, trainers should decide how often learners should receive this feedback: daily, weekly, monthly, quarterly, semiannually, or annually. As one way to gauge desired frequency, estimate the length of the training period. Plan to provide an appraisal at least twice: once at approximately the midpoint of the OJT and once again at the end. In a job requiring one week of OJT, for instance, provide a performance appraisal at noon on the third day and at the end of the fifth day. In a job requiring one year of OJT, provide appraisals semiannually. Thereafter, conduct appraisals in conformance with the organization's stated policies.

Level 4: Evaluating Organizational Results

According to a classic (and still relevant) approach suggested by Paul Brauchle (1992), who builds on the work of Terence Jackson (1989), the value of training may be computed in three phases comprising a total of twelve steps. Brauchle's approach is especially useful in determining the bottom-line value of OJT. It has the advantage of dovetailing with existing organizational compensation efforts to place financial value on work.

To apply the approach and thereby forecast (before training) or evaluate (after training) the economic value of OJT and the organizational results stemming from it, take the following actions (Brauchle, pp. 35–40).

Phase I: Determine Task Weightings

1. Conduct a job analysis (see Exhibit 9.4).
2. Establish a difficulty rating for each task (for example, use the rating criteria in Table 9.1).
3. Establish the relative importance of each task (see Table 9.1).
4. Establish frequency or time values, meaning "the percentage of [employee's] time that each task requires to complete."
5. Obtain difficulty/importance/frequency (DIF) products.
   • Multiply difficulty, importance, and frequency for each task (see first three columns of Exhibit 9.4).
   • Record the results (see the product column of Exhibit 9.4).
   • Total the products for all the activities.
6. Obtain DIF weightings by expressing the relative weight of each task.
   • Divide the DIF product for each task by the total DIF product for all activities.
   • Enter these weightings (see DIF column of Exhibit 9.4).
   • Total the weightings for all the tasks.

EXHIBIT 9.4. SAMPLE JOB ANALYSIS WORKSHEET.

Task	Difficulty Rating	Importance Rating	Frequency/ Time	Product (DxIxF)	DIF Weighting
1.	2	3	20	120	0.19
2.	1	3	40	120	0.19
3.	3	1	10	30	0.05
4.	4	1	10	40	0.06
5.	4	4	20	320	0.51
Total			100	630	1.00

Source: Brauchle, 1992, p. 37. Adapted from Jackson, 1989, p. 74. Used by permission of the American Society for Training and Development.

Phase II: Determine the Value of Performance

7. Record weightings from the job analysis worksheet to a performance value worksheet (see Exhibit 9.5).
8. Enter the worker cost (individual's annual salary or wages) on the performance value worksheet.
9. Determine value of each task by multiplying its DIF weighting by worker cost.

TABLE 9.1. CRITERIA FOR TASK DIFFICULTY AND IMPORTANCE ANALYSIS.

Rating	Difficulty	Importance
1.	Easy to learn. Little concentration needed. No knowledge of basic principles.	Of little importance to performance of unit. Errors do not matter.
2.	Some practice required to learn and maintain. Needs concentration. Some grasp of basic principles desirable.	Has some importance to performance of the unit. Errors may cause inconvenience.
3.	Constant practice required. Knowledge of basic principles essential. Decision making required.	Has major importance to performance of unit. Errors and failure to perform adequately may give rise to business or financial loss.
4.	Difficult to learn. Experience increases performance. High level of decision making and concentration required. Many factors and concurrent activities.	Unit cannot function without this key activity being competently performed.

Source: Jackson, 1989, p. 73. Used with permission.

EXHIBIT 9.5. SAMPLE PERFORMANCE VALUE WORKSHEET.

Task	DIF Weighting	Worker Cost	Task Value	Performance Rating	Performance Value
1.	0.19	$24,000	$ 4,560	1.25	$ 5,700
2.	0.19	24,000	4,560	1.00	4,560
3.	0.05	24,000	1,200	0.50	600
4.	0.06	24,000	1,440	1.75	2,520
5.	0.51	24,000	12,240	1.50	18,360
Total	1.00		$24,000		$31,740

Source: Brauchle, 1992, p. 37. Adapted from Jackson, 1989, p. 74. Used by permission of the American Society for Training and Development.

10. Establish job performance ratings based on supervisory assessment, committee work, or comparison with co-workers (see Table 9.2 for criteria).
11. Determine performance values by multiplying the value of each task by the employee's performance rating for that task.

Phase III: Determine the Benefits of Training

12. Compare performance values for each task before and after training. The comparison will show the dollars gained by investing in training (see the performance gain worksheet in Exhibit 9.6).

Brauchle's approach lends itself well to estimating the dollar value of training workers by task. It might be possible in the approach listed above to substitute the words *outcomes* or *outputs* for *task* and thereby emphasize the tangible results of work efforts.

Now it is your turn. Assume you have a worker with the data shown in the DIF analysis exercise in Exhibit 9.7. Confirm your understanding of costing out training by determining the worker's DIF weightings and performance value.

TABLE 9.2. JOB PERFORMANCE CRITERIA.

Rating	Criteria
0.0	Has produced no results in this function.
0.5	Has produced results in this function which are sometimes (about 50 percent) consistent with standards of quality and quantity.
1.0	Has consistently produced results in this function consistent with standards of quality and quantity.
1.15	Has sometimes (about 50 percent of work) produced results in this function which are well in excess of standards in both quality and quantity.
2.0	Has consistently produced results in this function well in excess of standards in both quality and quantity.

Source: Jackson, 1989, p. 73. Used with permission.

EXHIBIT 9.6. SAMPLE PERFORMANCE GAIN FROM TRAINING WORKSHEET.

Task	Task Value Before Training	Performance Rating Before Training	Performance Value Before Training	Performance Rating After Training	Performance Value	Performance Gain
1.	$ 4,560	1.25	$ 5,700	1.50	$ 6,840	$1,140
2.	4,560	1.00	4,560	1.25	5,700	1,140
3.	1,200	0.50	600	1.00	1,200	600
4.	1,140	1.75	2,520	1.75	2,520	
5.	12,240	1.50	18,360	1.75	21,420	3,060
Total	$23,700		$31,740		$37,680	$5,940

Source: Brauchle, 1992, p. 37. Adapted from Jackson, 1989, p. 78. Used by permission of the American Society for Training and Development.

EXHIBIT 9.7. DIF ANALYSIS EXERCISE.

Assume you have a worker with the following data. What is the worker's performance value? How much performance value was added by the training?

Task Analysis

Task	Difficulty Rating	Importance Rating	Frequency/ Time	Product (DxIxF)	DIF Weighting
1.	1	2	25		
2.	3	2	25		
3.	2	1	30		
4.	4	3	10		
5.	3	4	10		
Total			100		1.00

Performance Value

Task	DIF Weighting	Work Cost	Task Value	Performance Rating Before Training	Performance Value Before Training	Performance Rating After Training	Performance Value After Training
1.	_____	$25,000	_____	1.5	_____	1.50	_____
2.	_____	25,000	_____	0.5	_____	1.00	_____
3.	_____	25,000	_____	1.5	_____	1.50	_____
4.	_____	25,000	_____	1.0	_____	1.25	_____
5.	_____	25,000	_____	1.0	_____	1.25	_____
Total	1.0		($25,000)				

Source: Brauchle, 1992, p. 38. Used by permission of rht American Society for Training and Development.

OJT and the Balanced Scorecard

In recent years, much attention has focused around a so-called *balanced score-card approach* to evaluation. The balanced scorecard is a phrase that was coined by Kaplan and Norton (1996a; 1996b). Its primary application is focused around organizational strategy, noting that there is more to competitive success than mere economic returns. Kaplan and Norton posited that "success" could be examined according to a more balanced perspective. They suggested that, to apply the approach, decision makers: "(1) clarify and translate the vision and strategy; (2) communicate about the strategy and link it to goals; (3) plan and set targets; and (4) provide feedback on results and learn based on experience" (Kaplan & Norton, 1996a, p. 77).

A balanced scorecard approach to evaluating OJT would thus go beyond Kirkpatrick's levels to clarify and translate work expectations for individuals, aligning what they do or what results they are expected to get to organizational strategic objectives. Learners participating in OJT would then communicate about how their results are aligned to strategy and would set their own goals in ways linked to that. Working with their immediate supervisors, the learners would plan and set targets for their own outputs or outcomes. Finally, they would work with their immediate organizational superiors to establish a means by which to gather feedback on their results from customers and stakeholders and learn from that experience.

While much remains to be worked out on how the balanced scorecard approach could be applied to OJT, it fires the imagination by transcending traditional views of evaluation.

Summary

Evaluating results was the topic of this chapter. It is the fifth step in the DAPPER model. OJT is usually regarded as successful if the learner can perform essential job functions in conformance with measurable job performance standards under the trainer's watchful eye. Evaluation is important because it is the means by which training demonstrates the value it adds to the organization.

In Chapter Ten we turn to the final step in the DAPPER model. We examine how aids may be used to supplement, or even substitute for, OJT.

REVIEWING AIDS AND ALTERNATIVES TO OJT

How to Ensure the Right Mix of Performance Interventions

Planned OJT holds great promise as a means to accelerate the speed by which both training and learning occur in organizations. But it is no panacea. It will not solve every performance problem because it is inappropriate when the problem stems from a cause other than the performer's lack of knowledge or skill or the performer's poor attitude (see Rothwell, Hohne, & King, 2000). If the cause of the problem is rooted in factors beyond the worker's control, then other actions should be taken. At the same time, the trend is to consider blended learning methods rather than to rely on one approach, such as e-learning or classroom-based training.

Reviewing aids and alternatives to OJT is the sixth and final step in the DAPPER model. In this step, on-the-job trainers decide how much they can and should combine other training or delivery methods with OJT as aids to OJT, or whether they can and should substitute alternative methods of improving performance for OJT. Thus, the aim of this step is to double-check the appropriateness of OJT for solving a given problem and to enhance or revise OJT plans as necessary. In this chapter we review the OJT aids and alternatives that are available and provide advice about when and how to use them.

Determining Whether an Aid or Alternative Is Needed

Experienced instructional designers often rely on sophisticated media models to cue them when it is appropriate to use a particular instructional delivery method (Fowler, 1995). However, there are other ways to determine whether an aid or alternative to OJT is needed. Trainers can simply consider the four issues discussed in the following paragraphs and, if the answers they arrive at suggest that their OJT needs enhancing or is inappropriate, they can employ one or more of the aids or substitute one or more of the alternatives described in this chapter.

Convenience

Trainers should ask whether an aid to OJT is easily available. For instance, does the organization have up-to-date procedure manuals, computer-based training, interactive video-based training, policy memos, or other aids that might ease the on-the-job trainer's task? If so, using these aids can be a convenience for the trainer and can accelerate or enhance OJT.

Cost Considerations

Trainers should determine whether an aid to OJT is especially cost-effective. For instance, is it more cost-effective to supply learners with job aids—or even with training aids hard-wired into the work processes—than to invest wages for one-on-one instruction?

Time Considerations

Trainers should consider whether relying on an aid will save time for the trainers and learners. This consideration may be especially important in organizations in which on-the-job trainers are not readily available because employees are too busy fighting fires, handling crises, and getting the work out.

Learners' and Trainers' Feelings

Finally, trainers should ask whether the learners and/or trainers are growing tired of using the same approach for training on every job function. If so, they should investigate how variety can be introduced so as to maintain the interest of learners and trainers alike.

Aids to OJT

Over the years, trainers who conduct classroom instruction have proven themselves to be most inventive people. They have created many effective instructional techniques, including lecture, small-group in-service, demonstration, field trip, behavior modeling, case study, buzzgroup, critical incident, brainstorming, and role-play methods. Many methods of instruction have been cataloged to enliven teaching in classroom settings, and many of them lend themselves, with some modification, to OJT. Ideas for applying the ten major methods we have mentioned here are summarized in the following sections.

Lecture

The *lecture,* a planned presentation on a chosen topic, remains a common delivery method for classroom training. Lecture is usually an appropriate method of delivering instruction when the need exists to convey much information, especially to a group, in a relatively short time; the instructor is a subject-matter expert whose ideas are worth conveying to a group; key points or features of an activity, tool, or piece of equipment are to be addressed; or information changes so rapidly that lecture is a viable means of updating many people on the same topic simultaneously. Lectures can be used effectively in OJT when any of these same conditions exist, and it can even be used in one-on-one instruction, corresponding to Step 4 of presenting OJT, explaining key points (see Chapter Eight). Through lectures, learners who are beginning OJT can be given background information about essential job functions by their trainers, learning what the functions are, when, where, why, and how they should be performed, and how results should be measured.

Critics have long complained that the traditional lecture format has numerous disadvantages. Chief among them is that lecture casts the learners in a passive role; trainers speak while the learners only listen. Since learners can listen faster than trainers can speak, learners often grow bored when they are not asked to do something. Moreover, the learner's passive role flies in the face of recent training trends that favor increased learner involvement and participation that can make training more successful.

Nevertheless, the lecture method can be used effectively in OJT when appropriate conditions exist and when it relies on techniques designed to involve learners. To achieve learner involvement, trainers can ask learners to:

- Read about the job function or work-related problem in appropriate procedure memos, equipment manuals, or other written sources of information before a lecture is given.
- Prepare a list of questions and bring it with them to a lecture.
- Compile examples of problems or situations they or their more experienced co-workers have encountered in real situations.
- Work through a difficult problem or example, supplied by the trainer before the lecture.

- Survey experienced co-workers about the most common problems these work-ers have encountered.
- Complete a brief quiz or instrument prepared by trainers to surface gaps in learners' knowledge.

Small-Group In-Service Training

Small-group in-service training combines a short lecture with a few other instruc-tional methods and is delivered to more than one employee on the job. Although planned, it is rarely lengthy. For example, a supervisor, experienced co-worker, or other trainer might assemble a small group of workers around a desk or work station for an update on new equipment or a new work policy, procedure, method, or technique. In this kind of training, workers are usually told about the change, given a brief demonstration, and then given a chance to pose questions. It is an almost lightning-fast method of updating employees on changes occur-ring in the workplace and can be easily combined with a staff meeting.

Demonstration

A *demonstration* is an illustrated presentation in which trainers rely on visual aids or other props to enliven discussion and stimulate learners' senses in order to reinforce important points. In some respects, demonstration corresponds to Step 3 of presenting OJT, showing learners how to perform (see Chapter Eight). In demonstrations, trainers show learners both what to do and how to do it. To use demonstrations effectively in OJT, trainers should take these steps:

1. Begin the demonstration with a brief summary of the background ("I'm going to show you how to. . .").
2. Create illustrations or examples capable of being shown to learners.
3. Make sure that equipment, tools, software, or other objects or activities are in proper working order before they are shown to learners.
4. Present the procedure step-by-step, allowing the learners frequent chances to follow up—perhaps after each step—so they gain hands-on experience and their self-confidence is increased from that successful experience.

Like the lecture, the demonstration may cast learners in the passive role of observers unless trainers take active steps to give them hands-on experience.

Other techniques can also be used in OJT demonstrations to increase learner involvement. For example, trainers can have learners try out a procedure on their own before the demonstration so they fully appreciate the problems of performing it. (This technique should only be used with procedures that do not endanger worker health or safety.) Trainers may also pick bright learners and ask them to research the topic to be demonstrated, present a demonstration to the trainer, and then subsequently present it to co-workers. This latter approach builds learner self-confidence while reinforcing individual initiative.

Field Trip

Field trips, especially in the form of visits to other work sites, have gained attention because organizations are sponsoring these trips so employees can benchmark the best practices of other organizations as part of total quality initiatives. In classroom training, field trips are used as an experiential learning technique to show learners how others are approaching a problem, procedure, or situation. In OJT, trainers can arrange a trip to another organization, or to a different part of the same organization, so that learners can see how a job function is carried out in another setting or how the consequences of their work contribute to meeting customer needs. To design an effective field trip, trainers should:

- Plan the trip thoroughly, ensuring that proper clearance has been given for the trainers and learners to enter another work area.
- Clarify the objectives of the field trip so it is clear what the learners will be expected to be able to do when they leave the field trip site.
- Give learners a list of questions to be answered during or after the trip, a technique that builds learners' involvement.
- Brief learners on proper etiquette so they are courteous and do not disrupt the area they visit.
- Emphasize key points to be learned.
- Permit hands-on experiences whenever possible.
- Follow up with learners, encouraging questions and reinforcing policies, procedures, or work tasks.

Behavior Modeling

"Reduced to its bare essence," writes Robinson (1982, p. 2) in a still classic treatment, *behavior modeling* "involves learning by watching and practicing. The learner acquires the target behaviors by watching a 'model' demonstrate them on film or videotape, then reproduces those behaviors in an intensive guided practice." Behavior modeling is more often associated with the soft skills training used in supervisory or management development than with hard skills training. Examples of hard skills include effective equipment maintenance or job-specific procedures; examples of soft skills include high-quality customer service or effective supervision.

To apply behavior modeling to OJT, trainers should:

- Select appropriate job functions to model (for example, dealing with irate customers or conducting effective disciplinary interviews).
- Break the activity down into specific steps or behaviors to be demonstrated to the learners.
- Draw the learners' attention to the modeling episode ("I am about to show you how to handle an irate customer").
- Provide models of appropriate and inappropriate behaviors.
- Use videotape segments, if possible, to expose learners to models that have been carefully rehearsed and/or that are difficult to replicate on-the-spot on a continuing basis.

After modeling a behavior, trainers should encourage learners to practice the behavior themselves, so that their approach may be observed by the trainers and the learners may close the gap between watching others perform the behavior and doing it themselves.

Case Study

A *case study* is essentially a story, often based on actual occurrences, used for instructional ends. Long used in classroom training as a means to reinforce key instructional points or lead learners to make their own important discoveries, case studies typically contain enough information to describe a situation but not so much that learners are unable to focus on the central problems presented and their possible solutions. Adapt case studies to OJT by focusing the studies on job functions, work tasks, routine problems encountered during work, or important but atypical situations. Case studies should usually be written out, although trainers may occasionally choose to tell learners a "story" and ask for their suggestions about appropriate actions to take based on the training they have received.

Trainers may write case studies based on actual problems or situations that have occurred in the organization or in the job environment. In this way, OJT case studies can become important repositories of institutional memory, an important component in organizational learning, because they embody the lessons learned by experience that have since been absorbed by the organizational culture. Case studies should begin by describing who was involved, what happened, and when, where, and how it happened. Actual names and places surrounding a real case may be disguised to avoid embarrassing real participants.

Often, the actual cause ("why did it happen?") is concealed from the learners so they can have the experience of selecting appropriate troubleshooting activities. They can also be asked to recommend what to do to solve the problem. Many case studies are designed to end with a list of questions to be answered by the learners.

To use a case study in OJT, trainers should introduce the case study by explaining its purpose and desired outcomes. The learners should be told how long they will be given to work on it, where they should devote time to it (on the job or off the job), what form their responses should take (answers to a list of questions or a recommended course of action), and who or what they may consult in formulating answers about the case (Should they talk to experienced co-workers or even to selected customers or should they consult procedure manuals or similar information sources?).

After learners have worked through a case study, trainers should follow up by reviewing learners' responses. This follow-up is an ideal opportunity to emphasize key points and to encourage learners to gain new insights about existing work situations through questions about the case study.

Buzzgroup

A *buzzgroup* is a small team of learners who share common learning goals. In classroom settings, they are often called *breakout groups* and are formed to examine a case study, carry out a role play, identify a problem, explore solutions to a problem, apply a lesson learned in training, or perform other activities. Buzzgroup activities may be limited by time or may be left open-ended, often at the trainer's discretion. To apply this method to OJT, trainers must be creative, but considering the interest in team-based management that has swept U.S. businesses, many organizations are ripe for the use of buzzgroup methods in work settings. A learner may be given an assignment to research with others, such as co-workers, other organizational members, or customers. Alternatively, the learner may be assigned to a task force, a group of workers chosen to work on a job-related problem until they can recommend solutions to management or until their solutions can be implemented by themselves or other empowered workers.

Here are some tips for applying the buzzgroup method to OJT:

- Clarify the issue the learners are to investigate ("I would like you to gather information on the following problem . . .").
- Describe resources that the learners may want to consult as they gather information or research solutions ("I suggest you consult the current procedure manuals and visit with the following co-workers to gather information").

- Explain how much time will be given ("I will give you until the end of the day to complete this activity").
- Describe the desired results ("I want you to come back with written recommendations for solving this problem").

Once learners have completed their investigation, trainers should follow up on the buzzgroup activity by asking thought-provoking questions, thereby reinforcing key points for the learners' future reference and stimulating further investigation.

Critical Incident

A *critical incident* is much shorter than a case study, but the underlying idea is similar. Learners are given a brief (one-sentence to one-paragraph) description of a problem situation and asked to suggest a solution, course of action, or cause of the problem. Long used as a needs assessment tool (Nadler, 1982), the critical incident approach takes its name from an especially important (critical) situation (incident) that can make or break successful performance (Johnson, 1983). To identify critical incidents, trainers should conduct some background research, asking experienced workers and supervisors such questions as the following:

- What is the most difficult situation you have ever encountered on your job?
- How did you handle that situation?
- What happened as a result of what you did?
- How would you handle the same situation if it came up again?
- Why would you handle the situation in this way?

The results of this research can then be used to construct short narrative descriptions of similar situations, keyed to job functions or work activities. Here is a simple example of a critical incident that a learner might be given: "You receive a phone call from an irate customer at the end of the day in which you are asked to change the amount due on an invoice. What would you do?" The right and wrong answers are determined from the recommendations of experienced workers and supervisors for handling this situation. For right answers, trainers offer praise; for wrong answers, they explain the appropriate action and give additional training, as warranted.

When critical incidents are used, they enjoy strong support from experienced workers and supervisors because the incident's job relatedness is beyond dispute. Learners generally like them, too, because they make instruction problem-oriented rather than theory-oriented. Trainers often like them as well, since they are usually easy to write and use, whether in a classroom or in one-on-one instruction.

Brainstorming

Brainstorming, in its classic sense, is an activity designed to stimulate creative problem solving. Long used in market research and in classroom training, brainstorming activities usually consist of two parts: idea generation and idea evaluation. The two parts are usually kept separate by design so that evaluative efforts do not impede the free flow of ideas. To apply brainstorming to OJT, trainers pose a problem or situation to learners and ask them to write down as many possible causes for the problem or courses of action for the situation as they can in the short time allotted. Next, learners are asked to evaluate their lists of causes or actions to narrow them down. Finally, learners are asked to select one likely cause and/or recommended action, giving reasons for their choices, so that trainers may see how well learners approach tasks linked to problem solving or action taking.

Role Play

A *role play* resembles a case study in which learners are asked to act out a part that they have encountered or are likely to encounter on the job. Some learners may not like role plays because they feel artificial and some mental effort is required to assume and enact the role of another person. There are several kinds of role plays that OJT trainers can use. In the spontaneous role play, learners are asked to assume their parts with minimal preparation and are given no written descriptions of the parts they are to play. In the reverse role play, learners are asked to enact the role of a co-worker or customer and reveal (and come to understand) how that other person feels. In the doubling role play, three people work together: two of them play roles and the third observes. The observer may step into the action as warranted. In the rotation role play, learners play a form of musical chairs by rotating parts.

Although it might seem difficult to use the role play in OJT, it is not. Trainers must only take these steps:

1. Provide background information about what a role play is and why it is used.
2. Brief learners on what parts they should play.
3. Ask each learner to assume the role of a co-worker, customer, supervisor, or whatever is required.
4. Ask learners to act out the parts, perhaps with trainers serving as players also.

After each role play, trainers should debrief the learners by asking them what they felt during the experience and what they learned. If necessary, trainers may draw on co-workers as confederates for purposes of acting out the role plays in the work setting or a quiet setting near the job.

These methods can be even further enhanced when the responsibility for developing learning strategies is shifted from trainers to learners. For more information about how to do that, see Rothwell and Sensenig (1999) and Rothwell (1999b, 1999c, 1999d, 1999e, 1999f, 1999g, 1999h, 1999i, 1999j).

Additional Tools to Support OJT

OJT may be supported by other tools than those from the classroom. These tools range from low- to high-tech and include job aids, decision tables, policy memos and other written aids, procedure manuals, expert systems, electronic performance support systems, and virtual reality. All these tools may be combined with OJT or, on occasion, substituted for it. In the section that follows, we briefly review these tools and explain when they are appropriately used.

Job Aids

Job aids are best understood as performance support tools or devices that help people do their jobs in real time. They are widely found in daily life. Simple examples include labels, signs, troubleshooting aids, pocket cards, checklists, flow charts, and specific tools and equipment. Often, job aids are appropriately substituted for training when performers are not asked to perform a procedure frequently and thus have difficultly recalling how to perform it when it is needed, although the use of the job aid should not detract from performance, create a safety hazard for others, or pose a credibility problem for the user.

Constructing a job aid can be a simple task and frequently far less costly than providing training. The trainer need only (Pipe, 1992, pp. 361–362):

- Analyze the work to find critically important or infrequently performed tasks.
- Identify potential trouble spots in the infrequent tasks.
- Describe what goes wrong.
- Speculate why it goes wrong and then verify the cause.
- Find an appropriate solution to the identified problem.

The appropriate solutions may well include providing performers with job aids to help them perform, or aids for troubleshooting tough-to-solve problems.

As a simple example, consider the checklist as a job aid. Airline pilots use them all the time—not because pilots are incompetent but because they wish to be absolutely sure that they do not miss a critically important step in checking instrumentation before a flight. To develop a checklist, complete a task analysis, setting forth every step that an expert performer would conduct in the task. Then, turn the steps into a checklist, following a format such as the one in Exhibit 10.1.

Ask experienced performers to review the checklist before it is used. It may also be appropriate to conduct a behavioral task analysis in which the checklist is verified by acting out a procedure and revised if any step has been left out. Performers should know where checklists can be found, when they should be used, and where they should be filed for subsequent review upon completion.

Decision Tables

Decision tables are algorithms, understood to mean "precise procedures of demonstrated effectiveness in enabling the intended users to solve most problems in defined problem areas" (Horabin & Lewis, 1978, p. 31). Well-defined algorithms cue performers to start a procedure; define clear decision points when appropriate actions are or are not warranted; lead to a solution; and flow in one direction. The work-flow analysis in Figure 5.1 is an algorithm.

Decision tables are frequently based on if-then logic: if certain conditions are met, then certain actions should follow or should be taken. Trainers can set up decision tables to collapse quantities of information into convenient formats for performers to access as they need to. Use the decision table worksheet in Exhibit 10.2 to format such tables.

EXHIBIT 10.1. CHECKLIST WORKSHEET.

Directions: Complete the following checklist using a check mark to answer each question yes or no. Use the right-hand column to make notes. Do not skip steps without providing an explanation. When you finish, sign the checklist and date it in the space at the bottom of the page and submit it to _____for review and filing.

Did you perform this action?

(List each step in the procedure in this column, beginning each description with a verb.)

	Yes	No	Notes
1.	( )	( )	
2.	( )	( )	
3.	( )	( )	

I certify that the procedure was performed in compliance with the steps indicated above.

Signature   Date

EXHIBIT 10.2. DECISION TABLE WORKSHEET.

If *(condition)* is and *(condition)* is then perform *(action)*

List condition choices here	List condition choices here	List action choices here
_____	_____	_____
_____	_____	_____
_____	_____	_____

Mastering the Instructional Design Process: A Systematic Approach, Third Edition. Copyright © 2004 by John Wiley & Sons, Inc. Reproduced by permission of Pfeiffer, an Imprint of Wiley. www.pfeiffer.com

Well-constructed decision tables can cut down considerably on what learners need to be taught, particularly about routine procedures. Trainers need only familiarize the learners with where to find and how to use current decision tables. Of course, keeping decision tables current amid fast-breaking changes in work methods can be challenging, especially in organizations in which time and staff are in short supply.

Policy and Procedure Memos

Policy and procedure memos provide performers with specific information about how to handle situations or events or how to deal with changes occurring in procedures, equipment, or tools. Although these memos can help any job incumbent, they are particularly appropriate for experienced performers who have successfully demonstrated that they can perform all job functions in conformance with measurable job standards and have been released from OJT.

Policy and procedure memos may be formal or informal. Informal memos are common, even in small organizations. For example, a supervisor might send a memo to staff because a change has been made in a certain procedure. The memo may be only a few sentences in length, but it describes what to do in certain situations and how to do it. Conversely, a formal policy and procedure memo sets forth detailed guidelines for action. It explains what to do and why and how it should be done. If it marks a change in policy and procedure, it may also clarify who is affected by the change, what the change means, when it goes into effect, where it applies, why it occurred, and how it should be handled through revised procedures.

Trainers may use policy and procedure memos to document standard operating procedures (SOPs), asking newcomers in training to review the memos that apply to the newcomers' specific job functions or work activities.

Procedure Manuals

Procedure manuals, often designed in a looseleaf format, set forth the desirable steps in a function, task, or procedure. Procedure manuals usually provide more information and detail than job aids. Moreover, the process of developing a procedure manual can improve organizational efficiency because, if there are no SOPs governing routine operations, the process requires the creation of those SOPs. Although different approaches may be used in writing procedures, one effective approach is the *play script technique,* which takes its name from the resulting manual's resemblance to a theatrical script. To use the play script technique, write out the steps in a procedure from beginning to ending and indicate when each step is to be taken, by whom, and how. (If the results of task analysis are available, they can often greatly simplify the effort required to produce a procedures manual.) A simple play script procedure for answering a telephone is shown in Exhibit 10.3. Note that the "when" column contains the performance cue. It may list a date or an action as well as a stimulus, such as a phone ringing. The "who" column names the person who bears responsibility for taking action, and the "how" column lists procedures.

Procedure manuals can be immensely helpful as aids to OJT because they provide detailed guidance on every step of carrying out a job function. They can also facilitate ISO certification. However, they can pose more of an obstacle than an aid to performance if they are not kept up-to-date, which can be time-consuming.

Expert Systems

As Grabinger, Jonassen, and Wilson (1992, p. 365) define them in a classic description, "*expert systems* are an application of artificial intelligence that can be used to improve human performance." They can serve as intelligent job aids, helping to facilitate decision making in work performance evaluation, aiding in the identification and categorization of performance problems, and assisting employees in choosing from among a large number of options. Thus, expert systems are decision support mechanisms, resting on advanced technology, that

EXHIBIT 10.3. SAMPLE PLAY SCRIPT PROCEDURE.

When?	Who?	How?
The phone rings	employee	1. Lifts receiver no later than the third ring.
		2. Greets caller by saying "Good day. This is (company name). I am (employee name). How may I help you?"

can assist performers in carrying out their job duties. They are not based on algorithms, as decision tables are, but rather on heuristic logic. Consider using expert systems when tasks are narrow, involve verbal knowledge, and can be well defined. Avoid them when tasks involve common sense, reasoning by analogy, perceptual expertise, changing expertise, and complicated reasoning. Likewise, avoid expert systems when no two experts find it easy to arrive at agreement (Harmon & Sawyer, 1990), or when the organization has insufficient resources, including human expertise, to make them useful. Expert systems are gradually appearing in large organizations. They will eventually change the face of the workplace, and it is safe to say that, in time, they will dramatically modify what people will need to perform their job functions.

One example of an expert system might be apparent for those who call a computer manufacturer for technical support. Most workers who offer technical support are equipped with an expert system, which can be a computerized database that logs the organization's experience with customers' problems. In fact, readers might even have an expert system on their personal computers if they have a feature that permits them to troubleshoot system problems on the desktop. That would be a rudimentary example of an expert system.

Electronic Performance Support Systems

Electronic performance support systems (EPSSs) also rely on newly emerging technology. Although still in their infancy, EPSSs aim to provide job incumbents with performance support—often, although not by necessity, through computers—at the precise time they need it. These systems are neither purely technological solutions to learners' needs nor purely specialized approaches to instructional situations; rather, they combine elements of both to integrate information, tools, and methodology for users in real time. The best-known writer on the EPSS is Gloria Gery (1991).

Perhaps the simplest way to understand an EPSS is to think of it as combining four interactive components: a computer-based referencing system, an expert system, online help, and computer-based or assisted instruction. More complex configurations are possible, but the power of this fourfold combination is that it allows a user to obtain advice about decision-making options through online help; find information on a topic relevant to performance through the computer-based referencing system; obtain decision-making help through the expert system; learn about all these issues through computer-based instruction; and combine the four elements when gathering information, making decisions, and performing job functions.

Are electronic performance support systems for everyone? When they are conceptualized solely as creatures of computer-based systems, the answer must be no. EPSSs can be expensive and time-consuming to establish and to maintain. Each element requires a sizable technological investment in equipment, software, and programming time. Add to that the need to ensure that the system is built to accommodate myriad human needs, and the monumental effort required to build an EPSS becomes apparent. However, the principles of EPSSs may be used, even when a computer-based system is not. The central question that drives these systems is this: What can an organization do to improve its ways of making its performance support system—consisting of the four elements of information, training, technology, and decision-making tools—available to performers in real time? Related to that question are two others: How has the organization presently configured these four elements? How could the organization improve their configuration so that they better lend themselves to use by performers in real time? When these questions are considered, they can lead to changes that will create a high-performance work environment.

The potential impact of performance support systems, electronic or manual, has obvious implications for OJT. If performers have information, training, technology, and decision-making tools at their fingertips, they are freed from the daily pressures of mastering and carrying out mundane procedures that can be system (and computer) supported. That means performers have more time to be creative, finding new and more efficient or effective ways to make products, deliver services, or meet and exceed customer expectations. When an EPSS is available, OJT can emphasize these creativity, productivity, delivery, and customer-service issues, rather than the mastery of routine information, skills, and procedures.

Virtual Reality

Virtual reality takes different forms, but the constant idea is to simulate the real world so that learners can practice in a safe environment in which their mistakes will harm no one. Virtual reality, too, is at the cutting edge of emerging training technology. At this writing, the best-known applications of virtual reality are to be found in state-of-the-art video games in which players can put on a helmet and glove to participate in a simulated new world of strikingly vibrant colors, action, and special effects. Less elaborate versions of virtual reality involve holograms (simulated three-dimensional images that are also found in video arcades), computerized simulations, and simulators of airplane cockpits, tank turrets, or nuclear power plant control rooms. Software development tools are placing simulations in the reach of even novice trainers.

In virtual reality's most advanced form, players find themselves immersed in a world that resembles reality–thus the term virtual–where their actions have seemingly logical consequences. When applied to OJT on a widespread basis, virtual reality will permit learners to simulate performance, learn from simulated practice and experience, and see without risk what happens when they perform in new ways. Allowing learners the luxury of experiencing "what if" job performance scenarios may also open the door to enhanced performer creativity. The day of no-fault learner practice, provided via virtual reality, is not far off. Advancing computer technology and special eyeglasses that give users the capability to see the real world and television imagery simultaneously already make this practice technically feasible. It is already in use in certain military applications.

Is virtual reality a godsend to OJT? Probably not. Its use requires a combination of training and technological expertise that is still hard to come by. Additionally, at least at this writing, the technology is rarely easy, cost-effective, or genuinely necessary. But these daunting problems will diminish over time. Virtual reality has the potential of forever changing OJT, especially when combined with such other powerful performance improvement technologies as EPSSs or expert systems.

Researching Corporate Culture-Specific Competency Development Strategies

Many organizations have been embarking on competency development efforts (American Compensation Association, 1996) where *competency* means any characteristic leading to successful performance (Rothwell & Lindholm, 1999). Competencies can and do link up to organizational strategy. They can also be accommodated in OJT efforts–not as a substitute but as a way of supplementing and enhancing those efforts.

A *competency model* is a narrative description of the competencies tied to success that describes what should be. Competencies are measured by *behavioral indicators* (Dubois & Rothwell, 2000) that link up an otherwise vague characteristic– such as "flexibility"–with the observable behaviors by which competencies are demonstrated. The discrepancy between *what is* and *what should be* is a gap (Atkins, 2002; Miller, 2001). Gaps are of two kinds: (1) *strengths*: areas of unique competency in which an individual is regarded as expert or highly successful; and (2) *developmental opportunities*: areas in which the individual may need to build competence to achieve parity with the competency model. Individuals possessing strengths with particular competencies can be coaches, mentors, sponsors, or role models for others, although they may also build those competencies even further. But individuals who have developmental opportunities need to build their competencies. They can take responsibility for doing that, but the organization's decision makers can help by pinpointing the ways by which they can become familiar with the organization's corporate culture and build their competence within a unique corporate cultural context.

But what is competency development, and why is it worth doing? What methods can be identified that will build individual competence? How are these methods identified, and how can they be organized and implemented to achieve the greatest effect? This section addresses these key questions.

What Is Competency Development, and Why Is It Worth Doing?

Competency development is the process of building competencies. A key assumption of competency development is that most competency-building efforts occur on the job or through real-time work experience, rather than through off-the-job experiences such as classroom training. As people perform their work, they learn. That learning is associated with competency-building efforts. Increasingly, individuals must take charge of their own competency development and build their work-related expertise on how to do the work or else may build their process-related competence in learning how to learn (Rothwell, 2002).

Competency development is worth doing because people will learn regardless of what the organization does. However, visionary thinkers and organizational leaders realize that a significant competitive advantage can be realized if work experiences are managed to accomplish desired work results while, at the same time, building the bench strength of their talented performers. In other words, work experience can be managed to build individual competence.

What Methods Can Build Individual Competence?

Say the word *development* to most managers, and the first thing many will think of is training. Longer-tenured managers may think of participating in a classroom experience. Newer managers may think first of an online experience. But, in both cases, "taking a class" is a developmental strategy.

But there are many other ways to build competence. Taking a class may not be a preferred strategy. After all, many classes take place away from the job and thus at a distance from the place where the learning must subsequently be transferred and applied.

If you brainstorm on how you might be able to build your competencies, you might think of many other strategies as well. Examples of non-training developmental approaches might include reading books or articles on the topic, listening to audiotapes, talking to other people, surfing the web, watching video-tapes, and many more.

Generally, developmental methods may be divided into two categories. The first category might be called *generic competency development strategies*. These are widely used. They can be used regardless of the cultural setting in which a performer is situated. Reading a book or article, for instance, is a generic competency development strategy because it could be successfully applied to build competencies in a nonprofit organization, a government agency, or a corporate setting. Many resources are available to support the identification and application of such generic competency development methods. (See, for instance, www.learningnavigator.com/.) Also see print publications such as Davis et al., 1990, and Oebelein et al., 1999.

The second category might be called *corporate culture-specific competency development strategies*. These may vary, depending on the corporate culture within which one works. For instance, in some organizations it is widely known that most people who are perceived to be skilled performers have gained a successful track record in operations or in production. Strategies of this kind are called "corporate culture specific" because they are, like corporate culture itself, assumptions taken for granted about the places to spend time to gain visibility, acquire a widely known track record of performance, or otherwise "cut teeth" where it counts. One way to surface corporate culture-specific competency development strategies is to ask experienced performers what company experiences they should seek out to build their ability. For instance, in a retail chain, essential development may have to be obtained by working in a retail store.

How Are Corporate Culture-Specific Competency Development Methods Discovered, Organized, and Implemented?

There are three basic ways by which to identify corporate culture-specific developmental strategies: (1) analyzing work histories; (2) collecting information from job incumbents; and (3) building future scenarios. These may be used separately or collectively. Each warrants examination as a method by which to pinpoint competency development strategies that are of particular value in a unique corporate culture.

Analyzing Work Histories. One approach to identifying organizational corporate-culture-specific competency development begins with identifying a targeted organizational group.

Suppose, for instance, that you wish to know how experienced engineers achieved their current job levels. To that end, examine their work histories. Where did they begin their careers? What assignments or projects did they participate in? Across a group of engineers, can patterns be discerned that suggest that the most successful performers generally spent time with specific people (*who?*), performed specific assignments or projects (*what?*), performed over specific timeframes (*when?*), performed in specific locations or parts of the organization (*where?*), dealt in specific issues affecting the organization (*why?*), or achieved specific financial goals (*how much?*)?

This approach assumes that successful people in one organization tend to share some common experiences. Once they are identified, they can become a foundation for developing others through work experience. Of course, it may be necessary to *infer* what competencies were built through each experience.

Collecting Information from Job Incumbents. A second approach to identifying developmental strategies involves collecting information from job incumbents. That information can be obtained through personal or telephone interviews, e-mail or web-based surveys, focus groups, and other methods.

Take a simple example. Suppose you are tasked to discover on-the-job, real-time developmental strategies that would build the competency of "business writing skills." You might begin by collecting information from successful job incumbents about that skill. You might interview them (or conduct a focus group) with questions like these:

- Suppose you have been asked to give someone advice on how he or she might build competence in the area of "writing skills." Think of specific work assignments, jobs, task forces, committees, or other groups that you believe would be a particularly effective place to position people to build their competence in this area. Where would those places be, and why do you believe they would be appropriate?
- Who (what people) in this organization would you pair someone up with if he or she wanted to build competence in writing skills? Who are they, and why do you believe they would be appropriate?
- What kind of writing might be most important to learn about in this organization, and where and how could someone in this organization gain exposure to such writing? Why do you believe it is important?
- How would you advise someone to build their skills around the most important or the most common writing that people do in this organization, and how would you suggest they go about it? Why do you advise that?

- How would you measure successful attainment of competencies in line with the organization's requirements? Why do you suggest the measurement methods that you do?

Building Future Scenarios. A third approach to identifying developmental strategies may require you to forecast the future to determine what changes may occur in competency development. While such information can be obtained through personal or telephone interviews, e-mail or web-based surveys, focus groups, and other methods, it is also possible to do it through scenario building. Scenario building, recently popular in strategic planning, acknowledges that the future is uncertain but provides best-guess descriptions of what that environment will be like and what will be needed to succeed in it.

To that end, building future scenarios involves working with performers in the organization to create descriptions of what the future might be like. A common approach is to prepare a pessimistic view, an optimistic view, and a realistic/best-guess view of what that future might be like.

Once the scenarios are built, then pose these questions:

- In each scenario, what developmental tactics would performers need to prepare themselves for that future?
- Who should be involved in these efforts?
- What specific developmental experiences should they undertake to have the greatest impact on the future?
- How should those developmental experiences be planned, implemented, and measured?

Obviously, this approach assumes that the future may be quite different from the past—and that developmental strategies may have to be identified and undertaken in the present in preparation for the future.

Competency development is here to stay. Many organizations are building competency models and conducting assessments to identify individual development needs as they establish and use learning management systems. While many resources are available to help practitioners tap so-called generic competency development methods, many practitioners believe that the greatest value is achieved by identifying competency development efforts that are tied to the organization's unique corporate culture.

It is likely to be an area of growing importance as organizations struggle to solve the so-called *knowledge transfer problem* that occurs when members of an aging workforce retire and their successors may need guided experience to prepare for assuming more challenging work responsibilities (Pitt & Clarke, 1999).

Summary

This chapter was the final one that focused on the DAPPER model. Recall that there are six steps in the OJT process that may be easily remember by using the acronym DAPPER. The DAPPER model can be used by individual trainers in the absence of an organization-wide OJT program. The six steps are: (1) **D**iscover needs for planned OJT; (2) **A**nalyze work, worker, and workplace for planned OJT; (3) **P**repare planned OJT; (4) **P**resent planned OJT; (5) **E**valuate the results of planned OJT; and (6) **R**eview aids and alternatives to planned OJT.

In this chapter, the last one about the DAPPER model, we focused on reviewing aids and alternatives to OJT. In this step, on-the-job trainers decide how much they can and should combine other training or delivery methods with OJT as aids to OJT. OJT trainers should also decide whether they can (and should) substitute alternative methods of improving performance for OJT.

In the next chapter we describe six important success factors for comprehensive OJT programs that encompass entire organizations.

Part Three

Reflections on OJT

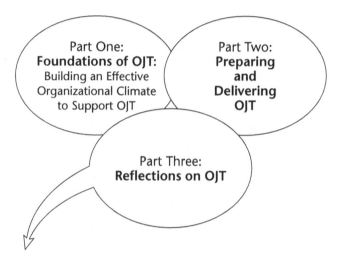

CHAPTER ELEVEN

SIX IMPORTANT SUCCESS FACTORS FOR COMPREHENSIVE OJT PROGRAMS

The six points discussed in this chapter summarize what we feel are important success factors for planned on-the-job training programs operated on an organizational scale.

Success Factor 1: Avoid Discrimination in OJT

Most on-the-job trainers are aware that discrimination is prohibited in hiring. Fewer realize that it is also unlawful in promoting, appraising performance, determining salaries, giving training, and other employment-related decisions. Organizations should take steps to avoid discriminating on the basis of race, gender, age, disability, or other non-job-related criteria in their OJT.

Sexual harassment, a form of sex-based discrimination, continues to receive attention in the United States, and the conditions under which OJT is often conducted may require special attention from organizations to prevent such harassment. One-on-one training, the most common format for OJT, can position two people in close physical proximity for prolonged periods and may make sexual harassment, or the appearance of it, more likely to occur than it is in other training situations.

Just as pernicious as sexual harassment, age discrimination is outlawed by the Age Discrimination in Employment Act of 1967, as now and herafter amended. Older employees are no less capable of learning than employees below age forty, although age does affect learning abilities in that older workers may have less "fluid" intelligence and more "crystallized" intelligence. Nevertheless, there is no truth to the old adage that you can't teach an old dog new tricks. Watch for issues associated with age discrimination to surge to the forefront as the global population ages.

Since July 1992, the Americans with Disabilities Act (ADA) has extended civil rights protection to the physically, mentally, and learning disabled in organizations employing more than twenty-five workers. Under ADA, employers are obligated to make "reasonable accommodation" for qualified individuals experiencing physical, mental, or learning disabilities unless such reasonable accommodation will impose an "undue hardship" on the employer or is justified on the basis of "business necessity." Nothing in ADA, however, obligates employers to demand less from any employee than full compliance with fair, measurable job performance standards on essential job functions.

To avoid discrimination charges, on-the-job trainers must be trained to treat individuals equitably. Even in nonunion workplaces, employers should establish internal grievance procedures to investigate and resolve discrimination charges. Employees should be sensitized through diversity training to the need to treat people fairly and should be cautioned against making comments or playing jokes that could be offensive to others. An organization's disciplinary policies on discrimination and harassment should be clearly spelled out, widely communicated, and vigorously enforced.

Success Factor 2: Enlist the Participation of Key People

An OJT program will enjoy the greatest success when key people in the organization play highly visible roles in it. For example, these key people can

- Serve on in-house OJT steering or advisory committees.
- Attend or help present train-the-trainer workshops to improve OJT and on-the-job learning.
- Serve as positive role models by setting good examples of OJT methods.
- Give testimonials about OJT methods used in their work areas and the benefits flowing from those efforts.
- Publicize OJT accomplishments to reinforce its importance.
- Permit field trips to and from their work areas or organizations as a method of supporting OJT.
- Provide adequate time, funds, staffing, and equipment to carry out OJT.

Success Factor 3: Encourage the Preparation of Current Job Descriptions—But Plan for the Future

To be successful, OJT must be based on current job requirements. After all, people cannot learn what they are expected to do if nobody is sure what that is. Additionally, studies show that supervisors and employees commonly differ in their ideas about as much as 50 percent of employees' responsibilities. Although current trends point toward the use of less formal ways than rigid job descriptions to assign job responsibilities, organizations must find some means to clarify and communicate essential job functions. While far from perfect, job descriptions provide a means to do that. Thus, they can serve as excellent starting points for OJT. These reasons alone lift them above the menial tasks they are sometimes perceived to be a part of and make them clearly worth preparing and periodically updating.

Job descriptions are also sometimes perceived to be restrictive, giving employees the impression that they are responsible for carrying out only the functions outlined on the one- or two-page summary that forms the job description. That limited view is neither always true nor desirable. Increasingly, employees are expected to contribute to work teams and cross-train for functions beyond their primary assignments. One way to deal with the problem of the narrow view is to explain to workers that they are expected to serve their teams and participate in training beyond their immediate jobs and to broaden workers' job descriptions by including these expanded concepts of the job duties in the descriptions.

Job descriptions can also misleadingly imply a static work environment. One way to avoid that limited perspective is to prepare future-oriented job descriptions, which outline employees' future job functions as they relate to organizational strategy and changing environmental conditions (Rothwell & Kazanas, 2003). These future-oriented descriptions should be clearly distinguished from their present-oriented counterparts, so that employees understand that the future-oriented documents provide only clues about the shape of things to come. Such forward-looking documents, however, do reinforce the idea that it is important for employees to learn job functions that they might be asked to carry out at some later time. These documents also place OJT on a future-oriented footing.

Success Factor 4: Integrate Internship, Cooperative Education, and Apprenticeship Programs with OJT

Employers are often willing to sponsor internships, participate in cooperative educational programs, and oversee apprenticeships for several reasons. First, they want to be good corporate citizens and believe that participating in such programs will lead to positive public relations. Second, they understand the value of strengthening schools at all levels so that employers will not face critical skill shortages or find major shortcomings with the students who are the products of those schools. Basic skill deficiencies are costly and time-consuming for employers to rectify. Third, employers find that students participating in such programs are often highly motivated, work only temporarily, and do not have to be highly compensated. Fourth and finally, such programs give employers the opportunity to try out potential workers before extending job offers. That reduces the chance that mistakes will be made in hiring decisions, and it may also mean that employer mentors can participate in preparing students.

Internships are practical and supervised learning experiences for students who are still enrolled in elementary school, middle school, high school, trade school, or college. Many educational institutions offer voluntary or mandatory internship programs to students as part of a program of study, with students receiving supervision from both the academic institution and an employer. Most employers insist that their interns work under a formal agreement established between the employer and the educational institution. Conditions vary widely: students may or may not be granted academic credit for their internship experiences, may be paid or unpaid, and may work scheduled part-time or full-time hours during the academic year or over a summer. Ideally, internships result in students who have real-world experience related to their academic studies, who are well-equipped to make the school-to-work transition, and who have improved employment prospects.

Cooperative education is both a mode of study and a joint agreement that facilitates employer-school relationships. Much like internship programs, cooperative education aims to give students opportunities to learn in educational institutions, apply what they have learned to work for employers, and then reflect on what they have learned. Cooperative educational agreements offer employers ample opportunity to shape the knowledge, skills, and attitudes that students bring with them to the workplace. In the process, employers can decrease the chances that costly training will be needed to rectify basic skill deficiencies.

Apprenticeship programs, among the oldest of all forms of training or schooling, are designed to provide planned, practical instruction over a significant time span. People often begin apprenticeship programs immediately after completion of formal schooling, although that completion is not always required. Apprenticeship programs are governed primarily by the National Apprenticeship Act of 1937 (as currently amended), otherwise known as the Fitzgerald Act. It is administered through the U.S. Department of Labor's Bureau of Apprenticeship and Training. The act permits unions and employers to be flexible in establishing requirements for apprenticeship programs so long as the programs are consistent with U.S. Department of Labor standards. To satisfy legal requirements, an apprenticeship program must include the mandated 144 hours of classroom (off-the-job) training and at least 2,000 hours (one year) of OJT.

Apprenticeship programs are an important form of occupational training, but employers often associate apprenticeships only with large employers, the manufacturing industry, the skilled trades, and labor unions, and that association has been a decided disadvantage for the growth of apprenticeships, considering that employment increases in the United States in recent years have been linked to small and medium-sized employers, service-oriented industries, unskilled trade and college-educated talent, and nonunion settings.

However, apprenticeship programs continue to receive attention because of the success stories pouring out of Europe (Northdurft, 1990), especially Germany (Bergstrom, 1988; Peak & Matthes, 1992; Robinson, 1990), about apprenticeship as a tool for helping the non-college educated become more employable. Apprenticeships can also be a factor in a nation's international competitiveness (Bas, 1989). Some have suggested using apprenticeship in conjunction with new, more rigorous certification requirements that are paired with high school diplomas as demonstrations of competence.

Numerous case studies describing successful apprenticeship programs have been published. One notable study describes apprenticeship at the Robert Bosch Corporation Automotive Group (Vasilash, 1990). Another describes a cooperative effort between the National Alliance for Business and the American Institute of Banking, in which apprenticeship served as a centerpiece for OJT efforts (Berry, 1991). Yet others describe success with apprenticeship at Westwind Air (Littlefield, 2001), Indiana Gas Company (Kelly, 1995), and at Digital Equipment Company (Lucadamo & Cheney, 1997).

Employers should take steps to become more aware of their potential responsibilities for apprenticeship programs and take an active role in designing, managing, and evaluating them. Numerous sources are available to support such programs (Cutshall, 2001). Employer involvement is essential because employer ownership of the concept is required to make apprenticeships work and to avoid plant shutdowns and other unfortunate consequences that may result when an organization's participation in apprenticeship programs is discouraged in hostile union-management environments. In particular, employers, and such other groups as labor unions and educational institutions, should pay close attention to the selection process for interns, students participating in cooperative education, and apprentices. They should ask such questions as these:

- How are participants in these programs recruited and selected?
- Who should participate in recruitment and selection efforts: labor only, management only, or management and labor jointly?

- What criteria should be used in recruiting and selecting interns, participants in cooperative education, and apprentices?
- What entry-level skills should prospective interns, participants in cooperative education, and apprentices possess?

The principles of OJT described in this book may be used in training interns, participants in cooperative education, and apprentices. To be successful with these groups, OJT should be closely monitored. Among the questions to consider are these:

- Is the OJT planned?
- Are measurable job performance standards established and communicated?
- Is the OJT documented?
- What will happen to interns, participants in cooperative education programs, and apprentices who are failing their training?
- How effectively will failing participants be counseled to help them improve?
- How much opportunity will failing participants be given to improve?
- What will happen if they do not improve?

Success Factor 5: Establish Measurable Job Performance Standards and Objectives and Link Them to OJT

Establishing measurable job performance standards is essential to a successful OJT program. Workers cannot perform well if they do not know how much, how well, or how often they are to perform or what is expected of them. Standards are the basis for measuring employee performance and determining how well individuals have been trained. Quite often the process of establishing, using, and communicating measurable job performance standards will lead to improved employee performance. That is hardly surprising, considering that "one of the commonly observed characteristics of intentional behavior is that it tends to keep going until it reaches completion" (Ryan, 1970, p. 95). People will work toward achieving meaningful standards–that is, goals–once they know what the standards are. Their willingness to achieve standards may be, in part, a function of the standards' perceived importance, the likelihood that the performer will benefit from achievement, and the performer's perception that the standards are achievable. In short, employees will obtain better work results if standards or goals are stimulating and the employees are involved and committed. The fact that people who face challenging job performance standards are more likely to achieve them is an important point to bear in mind in planning, overseeing, and evaluating OJT with any employees.

Certification can be a means of recognizing an employee's ability to perform at a level consistent with, at least, minimum measurable job performance standards. It thus recognizes competence in a profession, occupation, or job. The receipt of a certificate may document completion of training linked to job requirements. Certificates may be awarded by institutions when individuals complete a formal program of study, demonstrate proficiency by successfully completing one or more examinations, or show they can perform to a level consistent with fair and measurable job performance standards, but employees may be certified as competent without receiving a certificate or participating in a formal matriculation. Not to be confused with a license granted by a government that provides legal permission to practice an occupation, a certificate carries no legal weight. It demonstrates competence only to the extent that the granting institution can justify it based on occupational information and individual accomplishment. However, certification should involve at least a minimum demonstration of competence based on study and performance.

Certification relates to OJT in two key ways. First, learners should be certified at the time they are formally released from OJT. Both the employer and the trainer should be willing to show that the employee successfully completed a coherent program of study during OJT. Documentation for that program should exist, and the trainer should be able to verify that an employee is capable of performing at a level of production and quality that conforms to the employer's measurable job performance standards. Second, some observers believe that high school diplomas, and perhaps diplomas from other levels of schooling as well, should be awarded on the basis of a measurable and defensible demonstration of skill and competence. That movement has important implications because it suggests that employers may eventually be able to rely on schooling as a foundation for verifiable and identifiable entry-level skills that can then become the foundation for orientation, OJT, continuing education, and technical training.

Much has been written about certification in recent years. See, for instance, Hale (2000), Mosher (2001), Robertson (1999), and White (2002). McDonald's has even extended the notion of certification to include spouses (Arthur, 1999).

Success Factor 6: Plan for Cross-Training and Multiskilling

Cross-training refers to the training of workers to be backups for other workers, able to carry out jobs to which they are not normally assigned. For example, a laborer on an assembly line might be trained to supply the line with material, a chore normally carried out by a line serviceperson. When the line serviceperson is ill or is on vacation, someone must be prepared to step in and carry out that critical role; otherwise, the assembly line will have to be shut down. Cross-training meets an organization's need for a ready supply of trained workers by ensuring that someone is always ready to assume essential job functions. It is also the means by which an individual can be gradually groomed for movement from one job to others. Cross-training makes members of a work group interdependent and thus encourages teamwork. Everyone in the group becomes responsible for carrying out all essential job functions necessary for the group or team to achieve results.

Multiskilling is a possible outcome of cross-training. It encourages workers to take common ownership of the collective tasks of a work unit, team, department, division, or organization. Usually, *multiskilling* involves preparing workers to be capable of performing more than one job, so they are more productive individual contributors or team members.

Both cross-training and multiskilling have been pushed center stage in organizations due to widespread corporate downsizing and continuing interest in teams, employee involvement, employee empowerment, customer service, and total quality. Workers who feel common ownership in the job functions of others are willing to be cross-trained. They are also willing to help others when work demands exceed staff capabilities.

Cross-training is often viewed as the next step beyond OJT, so it is a fitting subject on which to close this book. Once people have learned their jobs through OJT, they are ready to be trained for backup roles for other workers or to be groomed for advancement. Many of the same principles applicable to a successful OJT program in an organization are also applicable to a cross-training program. An effective cross-training program for an organization should be:

- Governed by a written purpose statement and a policy and philosophy for cross-training.
- Established with clear program goals and measurable objectives.
- Targeted to appropriate employees, groups, or teams.
- Implemented through an action plan and schedule.
- Overseen at the organizational level by an identifiable person or group.
- Designed so that there are clear inducements to those who oversee it and participate in it.
- Explicitly budgeted for, if possible.
- Documented so that individual cross-training records are kept.
- Based on:
    Written and current job descriptions
    Essential job functions
    Measurable job performance standards
    Individuals' knowledge and skills that are clarified at the beginning of
      cross-training
    Written cross-training schedules
    The organization's strategic plan and individuals' talents and abilities

Although cross-training and on-the-job training generally share the same techniques and requirements, there is one important exception to that rule that occurs in team-based work organizations. In those settings, on-the-job trainers should develop team-based job descriptions, listing collective team functions, and those descriptions should be the basis for subsequent job analyses, individual learning plans, and cross-training schedules. In time, individuals may eventually be cross-trained for all job functions on their teams.

GLOSSARY

Activity. Part of a process; a discrete task; a manifest result of enacting a work responsibility.

Coaching. See *planned on-the-job training.*

Cross-training. Training workers to be backups for other workers.

Discrimination. Unfair treatment of an individual or group stemming solely from that individual's or group's race, gender, age, religion, ethnicity, or other non–job-related features.

Duty. An obligation to carry out action stemming from one's position or placement. See *job duty.*

Essential job function. A function that is "fundamental to successful performance of the job, as opposed to marginal job functions, which may be performed by particular incumbents at particular times, but are incidental to the main purpose of the job. If the performance of a job function is only a matter of convenience and not necessary, it's a marginal function" (Barlow & Hane, 1992, p. 54).

Ideal job candidate profile. A listing of all the functions or tasks of a particular job and the corresponding knowledge, skills, and attitudes that are required in a candidate for that job.

Incentives. Items or actions that encourage particular actions or behaviors. See *rewards.*

Job. "A group of positions which are identical with respect to their major or significant tasks and sufficiently alike to justify their being covered by a single analysis" (McCormick, 1979, p. 19). See *position.*

Job duty. An act or course of action required by the job holder's organizational position. Also, "a large segment of work performed by an individual. It typically represents one of the distinct major activities involved in the work performed, and consists of several tasks that are or may be related" (McCormick, 1979, p. 19).

Job function. An action or result that a job has been expressly designed to accomplish.

Job instruction training (JIT). See *planned on-the-job training.*

Learning center. A special setting for near-the-job training. Learning resources are deposited in a central location near the work area (Tuck, 1989), and learners access those resources as needed.

Measurable job performance standards. Minimum requirements expected from experienced workers performing at a normal pace. These standards–expressed in terms of time, cost, and quantity or quality of work outputs–are a means by which to hold workers accountable for performance and OJT trainers accountable for achieving desired results with their assigned learners.

Near-the-job training (NJT). Sometimes called vestibule training, NJT is the middle ground between off-the-job training and OJT. In NJT, learners receive job-related instruction in a quiet spot near the work area. For instance, a machine may be set up next to an assembly line, and learners may be given opportunities to practice on it before they are placed on the assembly line. In NJT, on-the-job working conditions, such as distractions and competing work demands, are minimized or only simulated. Training is thus realistic but does not slow down production or pose a possible health and safety hazard for the learner or other workers.

Off-the-job training. Distinct from OJT and often carefully planned, off-the-job training is usually designed to meet the shared learning needs of a group rather than a particular individual's needs. Classroom training is the most common form of off-the-job training.

On-the-job learning (OJL). What the learner does to acquire knowledge, skills, and attitudes in the workplace (not to be confused with OJT). Learners may acquire knowledge or skills on their own or with the help of on-the-job trainers or coaches. Most OJL occurs without the help of a trainer, and only some of it falls under organizational control.

On-the-job training. See *planned on-the-job training.*

One-on-one training. A training method in which one individual learns from another. Although most OJT is performed as one-on-one training, it is sometimes, albeit rarely, also conducted for groups, and therefore it should be viewed as distinct from one-on-one training. One-on-one training is associated with *coaching.*

Orientation. A planned program, typically conducted by a human resource department, in which new employees are systematically introduced to work rules, organizational policies, and employee benefits. Such off-the-job orientation is a common planned training program offered to employees in the United States. An organizational orientation program may be followed by more detailed divisional, departmental, or work unit orientations conducted by supervisors or co-workers. In this book, we assume that an orientation has occurred before OJT takes place. OJT should not be confused with orientation, although the terms may overlap conceptually.

Planned on-the-job training (OJT). In this book, planned OJT is synonymous with job instruction training and structured OJT and is usually referred to simply as OJT. It is planned instruction occurring on the job and during the work, centered around what workers need to know or do to perform competently. As Jacobs and McGiffin (1987, pp. 81–82) define it, OJT consists of organized learning activities "conducted in the work setting by a supervisor, or some other knowledgeable person, who demonstrates a job task to a trainee and then provides guided practice when appropriate." OJT may be overseen by a supervisor, an experienced co-worker, a subordinate, or a job coach from outside the organization, or it may be self-directed and thus overseen by new employees themselves. It usually involves one-on-one instruction (see Connor, 1988). While often associated with training methods for unskilled labor, OJT can be appropriate for any occupation or job level. When carried out for supervisory or management employees, OJT is sometimes synonymous with *coaching.*

Position. "The tasks and duties for any individual" (McCormick, 1979, p. 19). See *job.*

Responsibility. A moral requirement affecting an individual and leading him or her to carry out an action or act of duty.

Rewards. Items or actions that positively reinforce behavior that is exhibited or a result that is achieved.

Sexual harassment. Defined by the Equal Employment Opportunity Commission as "unwelcome sexual advances" occurring when "(1) submission to such conduct is made either explicitly or implicitly a term or condition of an individual's employment; (2) submission to or rejection of such conduct by an individual is used as the basis for employment decisions affecting such individuals; and (3) such conduct has the purpose or effect of unreasonably interfering with an individual's work performance or creating an intimidating, hostile, or offensive working environment."

Structured on-the-job training. See *planned on-the-job training.*

Task. "A discrete unit of work performed by an individual. It usually comprises a logical and necessary step in the performance of a duty, and typically has an identifiable beginning and ending" (McCormick, 1979, p. 19). A *job function* is typically made up of a number of tasks.

Tutoring. Remedial instruction provided to learners who need help to perform effectively. It is typically given to those who have been released from OJT but still experience problems in meeting measurable job performance standards.

Unplanned on-the-job training. Synonymous with unstructured OJT, unplanned OJT occurs on the work site but is not logically sequenced. Learners, typically new employees, are expected to learn by watching experienced workers perform or by actually doing the work. Unplanned OJT is "seldom well-structured, seldom based on well-defined performance criteria, and seldom time-efficient" (Sullivan & Miklas, 1985, p. 118).

Unstructured OJT. See *unplanned on-the-job training.*

Vestibule training. See *near-the-job training.*

Work analysis. "The process of obtaining information about jobs. Although this is usually done by a job analyst who observes and interviews a job incumbent to elicit the desired information, there are other procedures as well that can be thought of as some form of job analysis" (McCormick, 1979, p. 20).

Worker analysis. The process of obtaining pertinent, job-related information about individuals.

Workplace analysis. The process of obtaining information about the environment in which the work will be carried out.

REFERENCES

A three-pronged strategy to preserve critical training amid budget cuts. (2002). *IOMA's Report on Managing Training and Development, 2*(5), 3–5.

Al-Ali, S. (1996). An assessment of the on-the-job training programs in the ministry of finance: A case study of Kuwait. *Human Resource Planning, 19*(2), 50–53.

Albrecht, K., & Zemke, R. (1985). *Service America! Doing business in the new economy.* Homewood, IL: Dow Jones-Irwin.

American Compensation Association. (1996). *Raising the bar: Using competencies to enhance employee performance.* Scottsdale, AZ: Author.

Arkın, A. (1995). Training caters for special needs. *People Management, 1*(10), 32–33.

Arthur, J. (1999). A woman's touch. *Human Resource Executive, 13*(11), 72–75.

Aslanian, C., & Brickell, H. (1980). *Americans in transition: Life changes as reasons for adult learning.* New York: College Entrance Examination Board.

Assess, yes. (2000). *Lakewood Report on Technology for Learning, 6*(6), 3.

Athey, T., & Orth, M. (1999). Emerging competency methods for the future. *Human Resource Management, 38*(3), 215–226.

Atkins, P. (2002). Self- versus others' ratings as predictors of assessment center ratings: Validation evidence for 360-degree feedback programs. *Personnel Psychology, 55*(4), 871–905.

Atwater, E. (1992). *I hear you: A listening skills handbook.* New York: Walker.

Baldwin, T., & Ford, J. (1988). Transfer of training: A review and directions for future research. *Personnel Psychology, 41*(1), 63–105.

Barbian, J. (2002a). A little help from your friends. *Training, 39*(3), 38–41.

Barbian, J. (2002b). Screen play. *Online Learning, 6*(5), 12–16.

Barlow, W., & Hane, E. (1992). A practical guide to the Americans with disabilities act. *Personnel Journal, 71*(6), 53–60.

Barron, J. (1997). A structured comeback for OJT. *Technical and Skills Training, 8*(3), 14–17.

Barron, J., Black, D., & Loewenstein, M. (1989). Job matching and on-the-job training. *Journal of Labor Economics, 7*(1), 1–19.

Bas, D. (1989). On-the-job training in Africa. *International Labour Review, 128*(4), 485–496.

Benabou, C., & Benabou, R. (2000). Establishing a formal mentoring program for organizational success. *National Productivity Review, 19*(4), 1–8.

Bensimon, H. (1996). How to accommodate different learning styles. *Info-Line,* No. 259604. Alexandria, VA: The American Society for Training and Development.

Benson, G. (1997). Informal training takes off. *Training & Development, 51*(5), 93–94.

Berglas, S. (2002). The very real dangers of executive coaching. *Harvard Business Review, 80*(6), 86–92.

Bergstrom, R. (1988). What you've heard is true. *Manufacturing Engineering, 101*(4), 83–84.

Berry, S. (1991). Apprenticeship: A medieval idea wins a 20th century edge. *Management Review, 80*(8), 41–44.

Berte, L. (1989). *Developing performance standards for hospital personnel.* Chicago: American Society of Clinical Pathologists.

Berube, E. (1996). Mentoring is one approach to agent retention issue. *Best's Review, 96*(9), 82.

Bidwell, S. (1997a). *Helping students connect academics to the workplace: An implementation guide for student worksite learning experiences.* ED 411 440. Columbus, OH: Vocational Instructional Materials Lab.

Bidwell, S. (1997b). *Helping teachers connect academics to the workplace: An implementation guide for teacher worksite externships.* ED 411 439. Columbus, OH: Vocational Instructional Materials Lab.

Birchard, B. (1997, August). Hire great people fast. *Fast Company, 10,* 132–144.

Blackburn, R., & Hankinson, A. (1989). Training in the small business—investment or expense? *Industrial and Commercial Training, 21*(2), 27–29.

Bolch, M. (2001). Proactive coaching. *Training, 38*(5), 58–66.

Bolch, M. (2002). School at work. *Training, 39*(2), 50–54.

Boxer, K., & Johnson, B. (2002). How to build an online learning center. *Training & Development, 56*(8), 36–42.

Brandel, M. (1999). IT staff goes back to bootcamp. *Datamation, 1.*

Brannick, M., & Levine, E. (2002). *Job analysis: Methods, research, and applications for human resource management in the new millenium.* Thousand Oaks, CA: Corwin Press.

Brauchle, P. (1992). Costing out the value of training. *Technical and Skills Training, 3*(4), 35–40.

Brinkley, C., & Florian, K. (1998). Geneer specializes in "growing" people in a high-tech environment. *Corporate University Review, 6*(6), 36–39.

Brookfield, S. (1986). *Understanding and facilitating adult learning.* San Francisco: Jossey-Bass.

Brown, J. (1989). Why do wages increase with tenure? On-the-job training and life-cycle wage growth observed within firms. *American Economic Review, 79*(5), 971–991.

Brown, P. (2000). Learning from top-performing managers. *Performance Improvement, 39*(3), 16–21.

Brull, H. (1999). Start orientation on company culture when new hires enter your front door. *HR Reporter, 16*(3), 1, 6.

Cannell, M. (1997). Practice makes perfect. *People Management, 3*(5), 26–33.

Cannell, M. (1999). Tradition before technology. *People Management, 5*(7), 35.

Cannell, M. (2002). Class struggle. *People Management, 8*(5), 46–47.

Carlisle, K. (1986). *Analyzing jobs and tasks.* Englewood Cliffs, NJ: Educational Technology Publications.

Carroll, A., & McCrackin, J. (1998). The competent use of competency-based strategies for selection and development. *Performance Improvement Quarterly, 11*(3), 45–63.

Case study: OJT in action. (1994). *HR Focus, 71*(6), 13.

Case study: Tutoring production employees at Clorox. (1995). *Training & Development, 49*(9), 59ff.

Caudron, S. (2000). Learners speak out. *Training & Development, 54*(4), 52–57.

Charney, C. (1996). Self-directed peer training in teams. *Journal for Quality and Participation, 19*(6), 34–37.

Churchill, D., & Burzynski, B. (1991). More training with fewer dollars. *Technical and Skills Training, 2*(6), 11–13.

Clement, F. (1990). Accelerated learning models and techniques. *Performance and Instruction, 29*(3), 39–43.

Clement, F. (1992). Acclerated learning systems. In H. Stolovich & E. Keeps (Eds.), *Handbook of human performance technology: A comprehensive guide for analyzing and solving performance problems in organizations.* San Francisco: Jossey-Bass.

Conlin, M. (1999). Tough love for techie souls. *Business Week, 3657,* pp. 164–170.

Connor, J. (1988). *One-on-one/step-by-step: A supervisor's guide to training in the workplace.* Christiansted, St. Croix, U.S. Virgin Islands: TRC Press.

Cullen, J., Sawzin, S., Sisson, G., & Swanson, R. (1976). Training: What's it worth? *Training & Development, 30*(1), 12–20.

Cullen, J., Sawzin, S., Sisson, G., & Swanson, R. (1978). Cost effectiveness: A model for assessing the training investment. *Training & Development, 32*(1), 24–29.

Cutshall, S. (2001). Practical applications. *Techniques, 76*(8), 22–25.

David, M. (2002). Guide to successful executive coaching. *Info-Line,* No. 250204. Alexandria, VA: The American Society for Training and Development.

Davidson, O. (2002). How to choose the right coach. *People Management, 8*(10), 54–55.

Davis, B., Gebelein, S., Hellervik, L., Sheard, J., & Skube, C. (Eds.). (1990). *Successful manager's handbook: Development suggestions for today's managers* (3rd ed.). Minneapolis: Personnel Decisions, Inc.

Deming, W.E. (1986). *Out of the crisis.* Cambridge, MA: MIT Press.

Dent, J., & Weber, D. (1999). Technical training. *Info-Line,* No. 259909. Alexandria, VA: The American Society for Training and Development.

Desberg, P., & Taylor, J. (1986). *Essentials of task analysis.* Lanham, MD: University Press of America.

The dictionary of occupational titles. (1977). Washington, DC: U.S. Government Printing Office.

Dobbs, K. (2000). Simple moments of learning. *Training, 37*(1), 52–58.

Dobbs, K. (2001). Breaking through the fog. *Online Learning, 5*(2), 36–42.

Dobson, P., & Tosh, M. (1998). Creating a learning organization: Training and development in British Steel's universal beam mill. *Total Quality Management, 9*(4/5), S66-S70.

Dockery, K., & Sahl, R. (1998). Team mentoring: Boosts employee development. *Workforce, 77*(8), 31–36.

Donaldson, R., & Folb, B. (1999). An HR guide to catching falling stars. *HR Focus, 76*(7), 13.

Dubois, D., & Rothwell, W. (2000). *The competency toolkit.* (2 vols.) Amherst, MA: Human Resource Development Press.

Dubois, D., & Rothwell, W. (2004). *Competency-based human resource management.* Palo Alto, CA: Davies-Black.

Eline, L. (1998). International standards provide new niche for trainers. *Technical Training, 9*(2), 36.

Ellinger, A.(1996). Human resource development practitioners should strive for certification. *New Directions for Adult and Continuing Education, 72,* 75–85.

Ellinger, A. (1999). Antecedents and consequences of coaching behavior. *Performance Improvement Quarterly, 12*(4), 45–70.

Equal Employment Opportunity Commission. (1978). Uniform guidelines on employee selection procedures. *Federal Register, 43,* 38290–38315.

Evans, R., & Herr, E. (1978). *Foundations of vocational education* (2nd ed.). Columbus, OH: Charles E. Merrill.

Evans, K., & Metzger, D. (2000). Storytelling. *Info-Line,* No. 250006. Alexandria, VA: The American Society for Training and Development.

Fayol, H. (1930). *Industrial and general administration.* (The Coubrough Trans.) Geneva: International Management Institute. (Original work published in 1925 as *Administration Industrielle et generale.*)

Feldman, D. (2002). Distance coaching. *Training & Development, 56*(9), 54–56.

Feldman, D., & Bolino, M. (1999). The impact of on-site mentoring on expatriate socialization: A structural equation modeling approach. *International Journal of Human Resource Management, 10*(1), 54–71.

Ferman, L., Hoyman, M., Cutcher-Gershenfeld, J., & Savoie, E. (Eds.). (1991). *Joint training programs: A union-management approach to preparing workers for the future.* Ithaca, NY: ILR Press.

Fetterman, H. (1996). Certifying instructors in-house: An adaptable implementation model. *Technical and Skills Training, 7*(6), 10–15.

Filipczak, B. (1993). Frick teaches frack. *Training, 30*(6), 30–36.

Filipczak, B. (1998). The executive coach: Helper or healer. *Training, 35*(3), 30–36.

Flynn, G. (1996). Get the best from employees with learning disabilities. *Personnel Journal, 75*(1), 76–84.

Fowler, A. (1995). How to decide on training methods. *People Management, 1*(25), 36.

French, J., & Raven, B. (1959). The bases of social power. In D. Cartwright (Ed.), *Studies in social power.* Ann Arbor, MI: University of Michigan, Institute for Social Research.

Gale, S. (2001). Creative training: Doing more with less. *Workforce, 80*(10), 82–88.

Ganzel, R. (1998). Putting out the welcome mat. *Training, 35*(3), 54–62.

Garvey, C. (2001). The whirlwind of a new job. *HRMagazine, 46*(6), 110–118.

Gebelein, S., Nelson-Neuhaus, K., Sloan, E., & Lee, D. (1999). *Successful executive's handbook.* Minneapolis: Personnel Decisions, Inc.

George, M., & Miller, K. (1996). Assimilating new employees. *Training & Development, 50*(7), 49–50.

Gery, G. (1991). *Electronic performance support systems: How and why to remake the workplace through the strategic application of technology.* Cambridge, MA: Ziff Institute.

Grabinger, R., Jonassen, D., & Wilson, B. (1992). The use of expert systems. In H. Stolovich & E. Keeps (Eds.), *Handbook of human performance technology: A comprehensive guide for analyzing and solving performance problems in organizations.* San Francisco: Jossey-Bass.

Guglielmino, L. (1977). *Development of the self-directed learning readiness scale.* Unpublished doctoral dissertation. Athens, GA: University of Georgia.

Guglielmino, L., & Guglielmino, P. (1988). Self-directed learning in business and industry: An information age imperative. In H. Long & Associates (Eds.), *Self-directed learning: Applications and theory.* Athens, GA: Adult Education Department, University of Georgia.

Hale, J. (2000). *Performance-based certification: How to design a valid, defensible, cost-effective program.* San Francisco: Pfeiffer.

Harmon, P., & Sawyer, B. (1990). *Creating expert systems for business and industry.* New York: John Wiley & Sons.

Harrison, A. (1994). The selection and development of Indonesian graduates in an industry training program. *Asia Pacific Journal of Human Resources, 32*(3), 114–123.

Hartley, D. (1999). *Job analysis at the speed of reality.* Amherst, MA: HRD Press.

Hartley, D., & Stroupe, P. (1995). Comic books for technical training. *Technical and Skills Training, 6*(6), 16–20.

Hemp, P. (2002). My week as a room-service waiter at the Ritz. *Harvard Business Review, 80*(6), 50–62.

Hodges, T. (2001). *Linking learning and performance: A practical guide to measuring learning and on-the-job application.* Woburn, MA: Butterworth-Heinemann.

Homan, M., & Miller, L. (2002). Ace coaching alliances. *Training & Development, 56*(1), 40–46.

Horabin, I., & Lewis, B. (1978). *Algorithms.* Englewood Cliffs, NJ: Educational Technology Publications.

Hovelynk, J. (1998). Learning from accident analysis: The dynamics leading up to a rafting accident. *Journal of Experiential Education, 21*(2), 86–95.

ISO 9000: Handbook of quality standards and compliance. (1992). Greenwich, CT: Bureau of Business Practice.

Jackson, S. (1986). *Task analysis.* In M. Smith (Ed.), *Introduction to performance technology.* Washington, DC: The National Society for Performance and Instruction.

Jackson, T. (1989). *Evaluation: Relating training to business performance.* San Francisco: Pfeiffer.

Jacobs, R. (Ed.). (2002). *In action: Implementing on-the-job learning.* Alexandria, VA: The American Society for Training and Development.

Jacobs, R. (2003). *Structured on-the-job training: Unleashing employee expertise into the workplace* (2nd ed.) San Francisco: Berrett-Koehler.

Jacobs, R., & Jones, M. (1990). Job loss and dislocated workers: Description and opportunities for HRD practice and research. *Human Resource Development Quarterly, 1*(3), 251–262.

Jacobs, R., Jones, M., & Neil, S. (1992). A case study in forecasting the financial benefits of unstructured and structured on-the-job training. *Human Resource Development Quarterly, 3*(2), 133–139.

Jacobs, R., & McGiffin, T. (1987). A human performance system using a structured on-the-job training approach. *Training & Development, 41*(11), 81–82.

Johnson, S. (1983). Critical incident. In F. Ulschak (Ed.), *Human resource development: The theory and practice of need assessment* (pp. 133–151). Reston, VA: Reston Publishing.

Jonassen, D., Hannum, W., & Tessmer, M. (1989). *Handbook of task analysis procedures.* Westport, CT: Greenwood Publishing.

Kapfer, P., & Kapfer, M. (1978). *Inquiry ILPs: Individualized learning plans for life-based inquiry.* Englewood Cliffs, NJ: Educational Technology Publications.

Kaplan, R., & Norton, D. (1996a). *The balanced scorecard: Translating strategy into action.* Boston: Harvard Business School Press.

Kaplan, R., & Norton, D. (1996b, January/February). Using the balanced scorecard as a strategic management system. *Harvard Business Review,* p. 77.

Kaye, B., & Scheef, D. (2000). Mentoring. *Info-Line,* No. 250004. Alexandria, VA: The American Society for Training and Development.

Kelly, R. (1995). Apprenticeship training pays big dividends. *Technical and Skills Training, 6*(5), 22–24.

Kenyon, H. (1999). How do you train two million people? Manpower's answer is "log out." *Corporate University Review, 7*(2), 24–27.

Kiger, P. (2002). Why customer satisfaction starts with HR. *Workforce, 81*(5), 26–32.

Kirkpatrick, D. (1997). *Evaluating training programs: The four levels* (2nd ed.). San Francisco: Berrett-Koehler.

Knight, J. (1999). The school of hard rocks. *Training, 36*(8), 36–38.

Knowles, M. (1986). *Using learning contracts: Practical approaches to individualizing and structuring learning.* San Francisco: Jossey-Bass.

Kolb, D. (1980). *The adaptive style inventory.* Cleveland, OH: David Kolb.

Kolb, D. (1984). *Experiential learning: Experience as the source of learning and development.* Englewood Cliffs, NJ: Prentice-Hall.

Kovach, K., & Cohen, D. (1992). The relationship of on-the-job, off-the-job, and refresher training to human resource outcomes and variables. *Human Resource Development Quarterly, 3*(2), 157–174.

Lachnit, C. (2002). Hire right: Do it the Ritz way. *Workforce, 81*(4), 16.

Lahti, R. et al. (2002). Developing the productivity of a dynamic workforce: The impact of informal knowledge transfer. *Journal of Organizational Excellence, 21*(2), 13–21.

Laird, D. (1985). *Approaches to training and development* (rev. ed.). Reading, MA: Addison-Wesley.

Latemore, G., & Callan, V. (1998). Odysseus for today: Ancient and modern lessons for leaders. *Asia Pacific Journal of Human Resources, 36*(3), 76–86.

Lawson, K. (1997). *Improving on-the-job training and coaching.* Alexandria, VA: The American Society for Training and Development.

LD at a glance. (n.d.). New York: National Center for Learning Disabilities. Available: www.ncld.org/LDInfoZone/InfoZone_FactSheet_LD.cfm [last accessed September 4, 2003]

Levine, C. (1996). Unraveling five myths of OJT. *Technical and Skills Training, 7*(3), 14–17.

Lindquist, K., & Jones, D. (1992). Skill-based job analysis. *Technical and Skills Training, 3*(2), 7–12.

Littlefield, D. (2001). Doing their bit. *People Management, 7*(1), 30–31.

Lucadamo, L., & Cheney, S. (1997). Best practices in technical training. *Technical Training, 8*(7), 21–26.

Lynch, L. (1991). The role of off-the-job vs. on-the-job training for the mobility of women workers. *American Economic Review, 81*(2), 151–156.

Mager, R. (1997). *Preparing instructional objectives: A critical tool in the development of effective instruction* (3rd ed.). Atlanta, GA: The Center for Effective Performance.

Mager, R., & Pipe, P. (1997). *Analyzing performance problems or 'you really oughta wanna'* (3rd ed.). Atlanta, GA: The Center for Effective Performance.

Malcolm, S. (2001). Battling boredom. *Human Resource Executive, 15*(1), 62–64.

Marsh, P., & Pigott, D. (1992). Turning a new page in OJT. *Technical and Skills Training, 3*(4), 13–16.

Marsick, V. (1987). New paradigms for learning in the workplace. In V. Marsick (Ed.), *Learning in the workplace.* London: Croom Helm.

Martin, B. (1991). A system for on-the-job training. *Technical and Skills Training, 2*(7), 24–28.

Martinez, M. (2002, May). What is personalized e-learning? *The eLearning Developers' Journal,* pp. 1–7.

McCord, A. (1987). Job training. In R. Craig (Ed.), *Training and development handbook: A guide to human resource development* (3rd ed.). New York: McGraw-Hill.

McCormick, E. (1979). *Job analysis: Methods and applications.* New York: Amacom.

McDonald, K., & Hite, L. (1999). HRD initiatives contributing to women's career progress. *Performance Improvement, 38*(9), 35–41.

Meier, D. (2000). *The accelerated learning handbook: A creative guide to designing and delivering faster, more effective training programs.* New York: McGraw-Hill.

Mentoring takes off at Douglas aircraft company. (1996). *Work Study, 45*(4), 35–36.

Merriam, S., & Caffarella, R. (1991). *Learning in adulthood: A comprehensive guide.* San Francisco: Jossey-Bass.

Mezirow, J. (1985). A critical theory of self-directed learning. In S. Brookfield (Ed.), *Self-directed learning: From theory to practice.* San Francisco: Jossey-Bass.

Miller, J. (2001). 360-degree feedback: Improving the selection process all the way around. *Pharmaceutical Technology, 25*(10), 122–124.

Morrow, C., & Fredin, B. (Eds.). (1999). *Worksite mentoring guidebook: Practical help for planning and implementing quality worksite learning experiences.* Columbus, OH: Vocational Instructional Materials Lab.

Mosher, B. (2001). The seven steps to certification success. *Certification Magazine, 3*(4), 66–67.

Mueller, N. (1997). Using SMEs to design training. *Technical Training, 8*(8), 14–19.

Mullaney, C., & Trask, L. (1992). Show them the ropes. *Technical and Skills Training, 3*(7), 8–12.

Munnelly, C. (1987). Learning participation: The worker's viewpoint. In V. Marsick (Ed.), *Learning in the workplace.* London: Croom Helm.

Nadler, L. (1982). *Designing training programs: The critical events model.* Reading, MA: Addison-Wesley.

Newman, A., & Smith, M. (1999). How to create a virtual learning community. *Training & Development, 53*(7), 44–48.

Nilson, C. (1990). How to use peer training. *Supervisory Management, 34*(6), 8.

Northdurft, W. (1990). How to produce work-ready workers. *Across the Board, 27*(9), 47–52.

Norton, R. (1997). *Dacum handbook* (2nd ed.) [ED 401 483]. Columbus, OH: The National Center for Research in Vocational Education, The Ohio State University.

O*Net Online. Available: http://online.onetcenter.org/ [last accessed September 2003]

OJT in Japan. (2000). *Training & Development, 54*(8), 62–63.

Open learning is no closed book for Vauxhall. (1999). *Training Strategies for Tomorrow, 2*(5), 9–11.

Open learning keeps Reuters at the forefront. (2000). *Training & Management Development Methods, 14*(1), 911–914.

Patton, C. (2001). Cyber coach. *Human Resource Executive, 15*(3), 52–58.

Peak, M., & Matthes, K. (1992). Lessons out of school: The German benchmark in training. *Management Review, 81*(4), 54–57.

Phillips, K. (1998). The Achilles' heel of coaching. *Training & Development, 52*(3), 41–44.

Pike, B., Solem, L., & Arch, D. (2000). *One-on-one training: How to effectively train one person at a time.* San Francisco: Jossey-Bass.

Pipe, P. (1992). Ergonomic performance aids. In H. Stolovich & E. Keeps (Eds.), *Handbook of human performance technology: A comprehensive guide for analyzing and solving performance problems in organizations* (pp. 352–364). San Francisco: Jossey-Bass.

Piskurich, G. (1999). Now-you-see-'em, now-you-don't-learning centers. *Technical Training, 10*(1), 18–21.

Pitt, M., & Clarke, K. (1999). Competing on competence: A knowledge perspective on the management of strategic innovation. *Technology Analysis & Strategic Management, 11*(3), 301–316.

Plachy, R., & Plachy, S. (1993). *Results-oriented job descriptions: More than 225 models to use or adapt—with guidelines for creating your own.* New York: Amacom.

Porter, L., & Lawler, E. (1968). *Managerial attitudes and performance.* Homewood, IL: Irwin-Dorsey.

Prickett, R. (1997a). Essential toils. *People Management, 3*(22), 43–44.

Prickett, R. (1997b). Polished performers. *People Management, 3*(7), 34–37.

Prost, M. (2000). Insider advantage. *Human Resource Executive, 14*(4), 56–57.

Raimy, E. (2000). Fresh ideas. *Human Resource Executive, 14*(9), 58–61.

Ravid, G. (1987). Self-directed learning in industry. In V. Marsick (Ed.), *Learning in the workplace.* London: Croom Helm.

Robertson, R. (1999). In-house certification. *Performance Improvement, 38*(9), 26–34.

Robinson, A. (1990). The dual system: Vocational training in Germany. *European Trends, 4,* 86–90.

Robinson, J. (1982). *Developing managers through behavior modeling.* Austin, TX: Learning Concepts.

Rogers, C. (1967). The conditions of change from a client-centered viewpoint. In B. Berenson & R. Carkhuff (Eds.), *Sources of gain in counseling and psychotherapy.* New York: Holt, Rinehart and Winston.

Rothwell, W. (1996). *The self-directed on-the-job learning workshop.* Amherst, MA: Human Resource Development Press.

Rothwell, W. (1999a). *The action learning guidebook.* San Francisco: Pfeiffer.

Rothwell, W. (1999b). Preface. In W. Rothwell & Kevin Sensenig (Eds.), *The sourcebook for self-directed learning* (pp. vii-x). Amherst, MA: Human Resource Development Press.

Rothwell, W. (1999c). The Rothwell self-directed on-the-job learning assessment instrument (2nd ed.). In W. Rothwell & K. Sensenig (Eds.), *The sourcebook for self-directed learning* (pp. 181–190). Amherst, MA: Human Resource Development Press, 1999.

Rothwell, W. (1999d). The trainer's role in self-directed learning (pp. 3–4). In W. Rothwell & K. Sensenig (Eds.), *The sourcebook for self-directed learning.* Amherst, MA: Human Resource Development Press.

Rothwell, W. (1999e). The case study method reinvented for self-directed learning (pp. 157–162). In W. Rothwell & K. Sensenig (Eds.), *The sourcebook for self-directed learning.* Amherst, MA: Human Resource Development Press.

Rothwell, W. (1999f). The role play reinvented for self-directed learning (pp. 163–164). In W. Rothwell & K. Sensenig (Eds.), *The sourcebook for self-directed learning.* Amherst, MA: Human Resource Development Press.

Rothwell, W. (1999g). Learning by flowcharting (pp. 165–166). In W. Rothwell & K. Sensenig (Eds.), *The sourcebook for self-directed learning.* Amherst, MA: Human Resource Development Press.

Rothwell, W. (1999h). Learning from electronic mail (pp. 167–170). In W. Rothwell & K. Sensenig (Eds.), *The sourcebook for self-directed learning.* Amherst, MA: Human Resource Development Press.

Rothwell, W. (1999i). Assessing selected competencies for self-directed learning (pp. 173–180). In W. Rothwell & K. Sensenig (Eds.), *The sourcebook for self-directed learning.* Amherst, MA: Human Resource Development Press.

Rothwell, W. (1999j). Planning for self-directed learning (pp. 191–194). In W. Rothwell & K. Sensenig (Eds.), *The sourcebook for self-directed learning.* Amherst, MA: Human Resource Development Press.

Rothwell, W. (2002). *The workplace learner: How to align training initiatives with individual learning competencies.* New York: Amacom.

Rothwell, W. (2003). *On-the-job training: A survey of current practice.* Unpublished report on survey results. University Park, PA: The Pennsylvania State University.

Rothwell, W., & Benkowski, J. (2002). *Building effective technical training.* San Francisco: Pfeiffer.

Rothwell, W., Donahue, W., & Park, J. (2002). *Creating in-house sales training and development programs.* Woburn, MA: Quorum Books.

Rothwell, W., Hohne, C., & King, S. (2000). *Human performance improvement: Building practitioner competence.* Woburn, MA: Butterworth-Heinemann.

Rothwell, W., & Kazanas, H. (1990a). Informal learning in the workplace. *Performance and Instruction, 29*(3), 33–36.

Rothwell, W., & Kazanas, H. (1990b). Planned OJT is productive OJT. *Training & Development, 11*(11), 50–56.

Rothwell, W., & Kazanas, H. (1990c). Structured on-the-job training as perceived by HRD professionals. *Performance Improvement Quarterly, 3*(3), 12–25.

Rothwell, W., & Kazanas, H. (1999). *Building in-house leadership and management development programs.* Woburn, MA: Quorum Books.

Rothwell, W., & Kazanas, H. (2003). *Planning and managing human resources: Strategic planning for personnel management* (2nd ed.). Amherst, MA: Human Resource Development Press.

Rothwell, W., & Kazanas, H. (2004). *Mastering the instructional design process: A systematic approach* (3rd ed.). San Francisco: Pfeiffer.

Rothwell, W., & Lindholm, J. (1999). Competency identification, modeling, and assessment in the USA. *International Journal of Training and Development, 3*(2), 90–105.

Rothwell, W., Sanders, E., & Soper, J. (1999). *ASTD models for workplace learning and performance: Roles, competencies, outputs.* Alexandria, VA: The American Society for Training and Development.

Rothwell, W., & Sensenig, K. (Eds.). (1999). *The sourcebook for self-directed learning.* Amherst, MA: Human Resource Development Press.

Rothwell, W., & Sredl, H. (2000). *The ASTD reference guide to workplace learning and performance* (3rd ed.) (2 vols.) Amherst, MA: Human Resource Development Press.

Rubis, L. (1998). Show and tell. *HRMagazine, 43*(5), 110–117.

Russell, M. (1999). Online learning communities: Implications for adult learning. *Adult Learning, 10*(4), 28–31.

Ryan, T. (1970). *Intentional behavior.* New York: Ronald Press.

Schuster, D., & Gritton, C. (1986). *Suggestive accelerated learning techniques.* New York: Gordon and Beach.

Scribner, S., & Sachs, P. (1990). *A study of on-the-job training.* (Technical Paper No. 13.) New York: National Center on Education and Employment.

Seibert, K. (1999). Reflection-in-action: Tools for cultivating on-the-job learning conditions. *Organizational Dynamics, 27*(3), 54–65.

Senge, P. (1990). *The fifth discipline: The art and practice of the learning organization.* New York: Doubleday/Currency.

Sharpe, C. (1997). Successful orientation programs. *Info-Line,* No. 258708. Alexandria, VA: The American Society for Training and Development.

Sisson, G. (2001). *Hands-on training: A simple and effective method for on-the-job training.* San Francisco: Berrett-Koehler.

Skill inventories: Companies identifying, tracking where employee talent lies. (2002). *Workforce Strategies, 20*(3), WS13-WS16.

Skruber, R. (1987). Organizations as clarifying learning environments. In V. Marsick (Ed.), *Learning in the workplace.* London: Croom Helm.

Smith, L., & Sandstrom, J. (1999). Executive coaching as a strategic activity. *Strategy and Leadership, 27*(6), 33–36.

Smith, M. (1980). Measurement and validation issues. In J. Springer (Ed.), *Job performance standards and measures* (pp. 193–210). Alexandria, VA: The American Society for Training and Development.

Smith, R. (1982). *Learning how to learn: Applied learning theory for adults.* Chicago: Follett.

Stamps, D. (1997a). Communities of practice: Learning is social. Training is irrelevant? *Training, 34*(2), 34–42.

Stamps, D. (1997b). Learning from the Xerox experience. *Human Resource Management International Digest, 5*(5), 3–5.

Steil, L., Barker, L., & Watson, K. (1983). *Effective listening: Key to your success.* New York: Random House.

Sullivan, R., & Miklas, D. (1985). On-the-job training that works. *Training & Development, 39*(5), 118.

Thurow, L. (1992). *Head to head: The coming economic battle among Japan, Europe, and America.* New York: William Morrow.

Tichy, N. (2001). No ordinary boot camp. *Harvard Business Review, 79*(4), 63–70.

Tuck, J. (1989). *The individualized learning center: Life-long learning for business in the '90s.* (Audiotape #9AST-W7.) Alexandria, VA: The American Society for Training and Development.

Tyler, K. (1998). Mentoring programs link employees and experienced execs. *HRMagazine, 43*(5), 98–103.

United nations of employees. (1998, May). *Workforce Strategies, 16,* pp. WS25, WS28-WS29.

Vasilash, G. (1990). Where training is a way of life. *Production, 102*(6), 60–64.

Verespej, M. (1998). Formal training: "Secondary" education? *Industry Week, 247*(1), 42–44.

Von Hoffman, C. (1998). Setting the standards. *Inside Technology Training, 2*(10), 32–33.

Vroom, V. (1964). *Work and motivation.* New York: John Wiley & Sons.

Wachtel, J., & Veale, D. (1998). Coaching and mentoring at Coca-Cola foods. *Training & Management Development Methods, 12*(1), 9.01–9.04.

Walter, D. (1998). Training and certifying on-the-job trainers. *Technical Training, 9*(2), 32–35.

Walter, D. (1999). Train high-turnover workers with updated OJT techniques. *HR Reporter, 16*(4), 5.

Walter, D. (2001). *Training on the job.* Alexandria, VA: The American Society for Training and Development.

Warner, F. (2002, April). Inside Intel's mentoring movement. *Fast Company, 57,* 116–120.

Watkins, K., & Marsick, V. (1991). Toward a new theory of learning in the workplace: A focus on informal and incidental learning. *Journal for Research on Learning in the Workplace, 1*(1), 13–23.

Watson, C. (1979). *Management development through training.* Reading, MA: Addison-Wesley.

Weber, P. (1999). Getting a grip on employee growth. *Training & Development, 53*(5), 87–94.

Weech, W. (2001). Training across cultures: What to expect. *Training & Development, 55*(1), 62–64.

Westwood, R., & Johnson, L. (2002). Take orientation online. *Info-Line,* No. 250212. Alexandria, VA: The American Society for Training and Development.

White, A. (2002). Building an internal certification program. *Info-Line,* No. 250203. Alexandria, VA: The American Society for Training and Development.

Wick, C. (1990). Learning from experience. *HR Reporter, 7*(11), 5–7.

Williams, T. (1998). Job satisfaction in teams. *International Journal of Human Resource Management, 9*(5), 782–799.

Winkler, K., & Janger, I. (1998). You're hired! Now how do we keep you? *Across the Board, 35*(7), 16–23.

Younger, O. (1001). Benchmarking the training process. *Info-Line,* No. 250405. Alexandria, VA: The American Society for Training and Development.

Zemke, R., & Kramlinger, T. (1982). *Figuring things out: A trainer's guide to needs and task analysis.* Reading, MA: Addison-Wesley.

ABOUT THE AUTHORS

William J. Rothwell is professor in charge of workplace learning and performance in the Workforce Education and Development Program in the Department of Learning and Performance Systems, College of Education, The Pennsylvania State University, University Park campus. In that capacity, he oversees a graduate program in training and development/human resources and consults with organizations. He is also president of Rothwell and Associates, Inc., a consulting company (see www.rothwell-associates.com).

Having served as a consultant to thirty-five multinational corporations as well as public and nonprofit organizations, he is the author or co-author of many articles and books on workplace learning and performance and related fields. His most recent books are *Competency-Based Human Resource Management (2004)*, *Mastering the Instructional Design Process* (3rd ed.) (2004), *The Strategic Development of Talent* (2004), *What CEOs Expect from Corporate Training* (2003), *Planning and Managing Human Resources* (2nd ed.) (2003), *The Workplace Learner* (2002), *Creating In-House Sales Training and Development Programs* (2002), and *Building Effective Technical Training* (2002).

He holds a B.A. degree in English from Illinois State University (1974), an M.A. degree (and all courses required for the doctorate) in English from the University of Illinois (1975), an M.B.A. degree from the University of Illinois at Springfield (1982), and a Ph.D. degree in education with a specialty in human resource development from the University of Illinois, Urbana-Champaign (1985).

H.C. Kazanas is professor emeritus of education at the University of Illinois, Urbana-Champaign. He received his B.S. and M.Ed. degrees in industrial education from Wayne State University and his Ph.D. degree from the University of Michigan. He worked for ten years in manufacturing as a machinist and production supervisor and for twenty-five years as a human resource development (HRD) educator. He has been an HRD consultant for such well-known organizations as the U.S. Department of Labor, the U.S. Department of Education, the U.S. Agency for International Development, Motorola, Westinghouse, the World Bank, the United Nations Development Program, the International Labor Office, and UNESCO, and has worked in Asia, Africa, Europe, and South America. He is the author of eighty articles on education and HRD and of several book chapters and monographs, and he has authored or co-authored eleven books (one of which has been translated into Spanish and Arabic) on technical training in manufacturing and HRD.

Index

How to Use the CD-ROM

System Requirements

PC with Microsoft Windows 98SE or later
Mac with Apple OS version 8.6 or later

Using the CD With Windows

To view the items located on the CD, follow these steps:

1. Insert the CD into your computer's CD-ROM drive.
2. A window appears with the following options:
   Contents: Allows you to view the files included on the CD-ROM.
   Software: Allows you to install useful software from the CD-ROM.
   Links: Displays a hyperlinked page of websites.
   Author: Displays a page with information about the Author(s).
   Contact Us: Displays a page with information on contacting the publisher or author.
   Help: Displays a page with information on using the CD.
   Exit: Closes the interface window.

If you do not have autorun enabled, or if the autorun window does not appear, follow these steps to access the CD:

1. Click Start → Run.
2. In the dialog box that appears, type d:<\\>start.exe, where d is the letter of your CD-ROM drive. This brings up the autorun window described in the preceding set of steps.
3. Choose the desired option from the menu. (See Step 2 in the preceding list for a description of these options.)

In Case of Trouble

If you experience difficulty using the CD-ROM, please follow these steps:

1. Make sure your hardware and systems configurations conform to the systems requirements noted under "System Requirements" above.
2. Review the installation procedure for your type of hardware and operating system.

It is possible to reinstall the software if necessary.

To speak with someone in Product Technical Support, call 800-762-2974 or 317-572-3994 M–F 8:30 a.m. – 5:00 p.m. EST. You can also get support and contact Product Technical Support through our website at www.wiley.com/techsupport.

Before calling or writing, please have the following information available:

- Type of computer and operating system
- Any error messages displayed
- Complete description of the problem.

It is best if you are sitting at your computer when making the call.

Pfeiffer Publications Guide

This guide is designed to familiarize you with the various types of Pfeiffer publications. The formats section describes the various types of products that we publish; the methodologies section describes the many different ways that content might be provided within a product. We also provide a list of the topic areas in which we publish.

FORMATS

In addition to its extensive book-publishing program, Pfeiffer offers content in an array of formats, from fieldbooks for the practitioner to complete, ready-to-use training packages that support group learning.

FIELDBOOK Designed to provide information and guidance to practitioners in the midst of action. Most fieldbooks are companions to another, sometimes earlier, work, from which its ideas are derived; the fieldbook makes practical what was theoretical in the original text. Fieldbooks can certainly be read from cover to cover. More likely, though, you'll find yourself bouncing around following a particular theme, or dipping in as the mood, and the situation, dictate.

HANDBOOK A contributed volume of work on a single topic, comprising an eclectic mix of ideas, case studies, and best practices sourced by practitioners and experts in the field.

An editor or team of editors usually is appointed to seek out contributors and to evaluate content for relevance to the topic. Think of a handbook not as a ready-to-eat meal, but as a cookbook of ingredients that enables you to create the most fitting experience for the occasion.

RESOURCE Materials designed to support group learning. They come in many forms: a complete, ready-to-use exercise (such as a game); a comprehensive resource on one topic (such as conflict management) containing a variety of methods and approaches; or a collection of like-minded activities (such as icebreakers) on multiple subjects and situations.

TRAINING PACKAGE An entire, ready-to-use learning program that focuses on a particular topic or skill. All packages comprise a guide for the facilitator/trainer and a workbook for the participants. Some packages are supported with additional media—such as video—or learning aids, instruments, or other devices to help participants understand concepts or practice and develop skills.

- *Facilitator/trainer's guide* Contains an introduction to the program, advice on how to organize and facilitate the learning event, and step-by-step instructor notes. The guide also contains copies of presentation materials—handouts, presentations, and overhead designs, for example—used in the program.

- *Participant's workbook* Contains exercises and reading materials that support the learning goal and serves as a valuable reference and support guide for participants in the weeks and months that follow the learning event. Typically, each participant will require his or her own workbook.

ELECTRONIC CD-ROMs and web-based products transform static Pfeiffer content into dynamic, interactive experiences. Designed to take advantage of the searchability, automation, and ease-of-use that technology provides, our e-products bring convenience and immediate accessibility to your workspace.

METHODOLOGIES

CASE STUDY A presentation, in narrative form, of an actual event that has occurred inside an organization. Case studies are not prescriptive, nor are they used to prove a point; they are designed to develop critical analysis and decision-making skills. A case study has a specific time frame, specifies a sequence of events, is narrative in structure, and contains a plot structure—an issue (what should be/have been done?). Use case studies when the goal is to enable participants to apply previously learned theories to the circumstances in the case, decide what is pertinent, identify the real issues, decide what should have been done, and develop a plan of action.

ENERGIZER A short activity that develops readiness for the next session or learning event. Energizers are most commonly used after a break or lunch to stimulate or refocus the group. Many involve some form of physical activity, so they are a useful way to counter post-lunch lethargy. Other uses include transitioning from one topic to another, where "mental" distancing is important.

EXPERIENTIAL LEARNING ACTIVITY (ELA) A facilitator-led intervention that moves participants through the learning cycle from experience to application (also known as a Structured Experience). ELAs are carefully thought-out designs in which there is a definite learning purpose and intended outcome. Each step—everything that participants do during the activity—facilitates the accomplishment of the stated goal. Each ELA includes complete instructions for facilitating the intervention and a clear statement of goals, suggested group size and timing, materials required, an explanation of the process, and, where appropriate, possible variations to the activity. (For more detail on Experiential Learning Activities, see the Introduction to the *Reference Guide to Handbooks and Annuals*, 1999 edition, Pfeiffer, San Francisco.)

GAME A group activity that has the purpose of fostering team spirit and togetherness in addition to the achievement of a pre-stated goal. Usually contrived—undertaking a desert expedition, for example—this type of learning method offers an engaging means for participants to demonstrate and practice business and interpersonal skills. Games are effective for team building and personal development mainly because the goal is subordinate to the process—the means through which participants reach decisions, collaborate, communicate, and generate trust and understanding. Games often engage teams in "friendly" competition.

ICEBREAKER A (usually) short activity designed to help participants overcome initial anxiety in a training session and/or to acquaint the participants with one another. An icebreaker can be a fun activity or can be tied to specific topics or training goals. While a useful tool in itself, the icebreaker comes into its own in situations where tension or resistance exists within a group.

INSTRUMENT A device used to assess, appraise, evaluate, describe, classify, and summarize various aspects of human behavior. The term used to describe an instrument depends primarily on its format and purpose. These terms include survey, questionnaire, inventory, diagnostic, survey, and poll. Some uses of instruments include providing instrumental feedback to group members, studying here-and-now processes or functioning within a group, manipulating group composition, and evaluating outcomes of training and other interventions.

Instruments are popular in the training and HR field because, in general, more growth can occur if an individual is provided with a method for focusing specifically on his or her own behavior. Instruments also are used to obtain information that will serve as a basis for change and to assist in workforce planning efforts.

Paper-and-pencil tests still dominate the instrument landscape with a typical package comprising a facilitator's guide, which offers advice on administering the instrument and interpreting the collected data, and an initial set of instruments. Additional instruments are available separately. Pfeiffer, though, is investing heavily in e-instruments. Electronic instrumentation provides effortless distribution and, for larger groups particularly, offers advantages over paper-and-pencil tests in the time it takes to analyze data and provide feedback.

LECTURETTE A short talk that provides an explanation of a principle, model, or process that is pertinent to the participants' current learning needs. A lecturette is intended to establish a common language bond between the trainer and the participants by providing a mutual frame of reference. Use a lecturette as an introduction to a group activity or event, as an interjection during an event, or as a handout.

MODEL A graphic depiction of a system or process and the relationship among its elements. Models provide a frame of reference and something more tangible, and more easily remembered, than a verbal explanation. They also give participants something to "go on," enabling them to track their own progress as they experience the dynamics, processes, and relationships being depicted in the model.

ROLE PLAY A technique in which people assume a role in a situation/scenario: a customer service rep in an angry-customer exchange, for example. The way in which the role is approached is then discussed and feedback is offered. The role play is often repeated using a different approach and/or incorporating changes made based on feedback received. In other words, role playing is a spontaneous interaction involving realistic behavior under artificial (and safe) conditions.

SIMULATION A methodology for understanding the interrelationships among components of a system or process. Simulations differ from games in that they test or use a model that depicts or mirrors some aspect of reality in form, if not necessarily in content. Learning occurs by studying the effects of change on one or more factors of the model. Simulations are commonly used to test hypotheses about what happens in a system—often referred to as "what if?" analysis—or to examine best-case/worst-case scenarios.

THEORY A presentation of an idea from a conjectural perspective. Theories are useful because they encourage us to examine behavior and phenomena through a different lens.

TOPICS

The twin goals of providing effective and practical solutions for workforce training and organization development and meeting the educational needs of training and human resource professionals shape Pfeiffer's publishing program. Core topics include the following:

   Leadership & Management
   Communication & Presentation
   Coaching & Mentoring
   Training & Development
   e-Learning
   Teams & Collaboration
   OD & Strategic Planning
   Human Resources
   Consulting

What will you find on pfeiffer.com?

- The best in workplace performance solutions for training and HR professionals

- Downloadable training tools, exercises, and content

- Web-exclusive offers

- Training tips, articles, and news

- Seamless on-line ordering

- Author guidelines, information on becoming a Pfeiffer Affiliate, and much more

Discover more at www.pfeiffer.com

Customer Care

Have a question, comment, or suggestion? Contact us! We value your feedback and we want to hear from you.

For questions about this or other Pfeiffer products, you may contact us by:

E-mail: **customer@wiley.com**

Mail: **Customer Care Wiley/Pfeiffer**
10475 Crosspoint Blvd.
Indianapolis, IN 46256

Phone: **(US) 800-274-4434** (Outside the US: 317-572-3985)

Fax: **(US) 800-569-0443** (Outside the US: 317-572-4002)

To order additional copies of this title or to browse other Pfeiffer products, visit us online at **www.pfeiffer.com**.

For **Technical Support** questions call **(800) 274-4434**.

For author guidelines, log on to www.pfeiffer.com and click on "Resources for Authors."

If you are . . .

A **college bookstore, a professor, an instructor, or work in higher education** and you'd like to place an order or request an exam copy, please contact jbreview@wiley.com.

A **general retail bookseller** and you'd like to establish an account or speak to a local sales representative, contact Melissa Grecco at 201-748-6267 or mgrecco@wiley.com.

An **exclusively on-line bookseller**, contact Amy Blanchard at 530-756-9456 or ablanchard @wiley.com or Jennifer Johnson at 206-568-3883 or jjohnson@wiley.com, both of our Online Sales department.

A **librarian or library representative**, contact John Chambers in our Library Sales department at 201-748-6291 or jchamber@wiley.com.

A **reseller, training company/consultant, or corporate trainer**, contact Charles Regan in our Special Sales department at 201-748-6553 or cregan@wiley.com.

A **specialty retail distributor** (includes specialty gift stores, museum shops, and corporate bulk sales), contact Kim Hendrickson in our Special Sales department at 201-748-6037 or khendric@wiley.com.

Purchasing for the **Federal government**, contact Ron Cunningham in our Special Sales department at 317-572-3053 or rcunning@wiley.com.

Purchasing for a **State or Local government**, contact Charles Regan in our Special Sales department at 201-748-6553 or cregan@wiley.com.